REPARATIONS
Sins *of* America

ANEB JAH RASTA SENSAS-UTCHA NEFER I

 www.trafford.com

North America & international
toll-free: 1 888 232 4444 (USA & Canada)
fax: 812 355 4082

First of all, in order of understanding the title of this book {Reparations - Sins of America} you must understand the English - Latin word usage of certain forms of syllables and phonetic usages therof.

Indeed, the prefix in reparation is re. Re means backward motion, refurbish, redeem and repetition.Therefore; if the following is correct, then there are unusual solutions to these unusual circumstances. You see, reparation within its own meaning is equated as the reparing of something, someone or certain diharmonizing conditions. This also means to make amends for a wrong doing or wrongs that someone or a particular group of people has done unto the True God or his Divine Beings.

This is done by paying money or otherwise helping those who have been wronged by you, your culture, your religion or your superior rank. Whereas: they have been victims of scoffer-mongering and pridefuls individuals who pride themselves into the sacrificing of the meager within their lower beings.

For example; In Islam - they do deeds in seeking forgiveness from Allah. In christianity, they are often in prayer for reconciliational forgiveness. In Egyptian and other eastern cultural religions, there are ritualistic tasks that coincide with forms of enchantment through mediumistic forms of self-empowerment invocational rites of the spiritalists. In this: you must really ask yourselves the following questions - are they actually seeking forgiveness - and true benovolence - or are they manipulating {YOUR BEING} through forms of various methods of ritualistic neurological sciences as if you were a newborn. This also includes pattern of transgenic organismic shaping factors. Whereas: these mechanisms will eventually deteriorate the following:

A: Central nervous system

B. Neurotransmitters

C: Within each of your 5 Brains

D. Autonomic Nervous System

E. Periphreal Nervous System

In their fulfillment process. They diviner(s) invoke seductive forms that includes delusions and swayness within weak and the spiritually unenlightened. They become slaves unto the ungodly. Whereas:

SIN:

Sin is an immoral act or immoral acts against of transgression against the unversal laws of divinity. Therefore: Sin{S} are crimes against the True God and His True Ancestry. These are crimes of intrusiveness. Whereas: they {Gods Ancesty-TRUE} assisted God in the creational process of governing the entire universe. This confirms the traces of necessary amends - reparations that are to be rewarded backwards. All have sinned! Find glory within yourselves. This Means that prior to any immigrants entering The United States of America and its So-Called Indian Natives, the commencement of slavery throughout the entire universe, planets as well as in America God's plan was in effect.

This is to say that this includes the following eras; Jim Crow Eras, Political Reconstruction and Civil Rights Eras that occurred towards the conclusion of the 19th and the Mid Twentieth Centuries within the United States of America.

You see:

Transgenic Organisms

Effiminization and Masculation of Every Organism & The Atrazine Chemical

As the development of Transgenetic Organism began - so-did the implementational processes of political infrastructuring. In this philosophical and pseudo-intellectualisms. Whereas: The majority of religions were written based on Supremacy methods as to emasculate the male and to masculate the femal. ; emasculation of the colored / minority male and masculation of females must cease. Whereas; all minorities of all social classes are owed reparations for the atrocities against them. America has never apologized for countless atrocities against anyone. This is due to its unexcused and false foreign policies on immigration, discrimination and civil liberties. It has been reestablished to keep us in their peculiar institution of slavery. The indians too were slavers of the African and African American. Of course, we must fix and reform through restoring ourselves through a spiritual awakening.

You see, we've been blind-sided by their darkness of plagarism and lies. Their lies also include inconsistencies and twisted forms of conditioned behaviors of beligerant emotions of lewness. Truly, we must become more independent than we once were in ancient Kemet. Indeed, have you known or gained knowledge of the Zero Dynasty. That will come later.

Moving right along. Job 26:10 He marks the horizons on the face of the waters for a boundary of light and darkness. Therefore; we've made a covenant with a government of sheol. Whereas; slavery was abolished in Mexico by its president, Vincente Guerrero before The Civil War and

1

the 13th Amendment of The United States of America were established. Napoleon and Joseph Bonaparte invasion of Spain in 1808 slaughtered the Moor as well Creole nations. In this; light and darkness is a representation of good and evil affairs of the Egyptologist and White race spy out the liberty of all people. Mainly, the people of color. If you have studied Job, you'll understand his trials and tribulations throughout his entire life.

Man has been effiminized as a result of the White man along with multiculturalistic forms of trangenetic transformation. This is an attempt to save himself along with his entire clan - tribe of spiritual deceitfulness from the employment of his will. His arrogance has made him collapse as a if it were the London Bridge. In addition; The Hobbs Act of 1951 that was established by Samuel Hobbs, which introduced a bill that would have made it legal to wiretap individuals who were a threat to the security of law enforcement as well as others failed to supply equality for people of color. Consequently, the system of powers has purged against itself. Ecc 7:26 Amerika is a woman who's a trap and inequality of civil rights is within her net. Whereas; we've become immune to being rated as second class citizens by all means necessary and headed backwards towards the boundary of darkness.

In addition; The Indo-European group of Hyksos' invasian of ancient Kemit has severed the soul of the American Culture through its continued epigenitic scheme of racism. Whereas; their initial plan was to dehumanize the African race til this modern day of unconstitutional folly is conquered with dignity. Where is the wise and disputing counselmen of this age? In addition; throughout the systemic racial methods that have been birthed within the United States Dept. of Education, which has mandated that Christopher Columbus' discovery of the America's is holistic in nature be taught within our education system of dogma and propaganda. In addition; there were wars of Grenada that occurred in 1492. This included the Moors. Note; many have awakend and risen towards the understanding that nobleman, Abu Bakari navigated the americas'. In addition; Christianity claimed credit as it warred with Islam after it (Greece) undermind the origins of Kemet.

Collosae 2:16 which appears to reveal a so-called "shadow" of things to come also reveals the following; do not let anyone judge you by what you eat or drink, or with regards to religious festival or a new moon ritual. You see; first of all; Collosae was of the Asia Minor and it was too a region of idolatry and paganism along with the Roman Republic which assisted in the adoption of the U.S. Constitution in 1787. In addition; the symbolism of America is symbolic to the very {Egypt} of which it denounces within its constitution as well as it religious doctrine.

Whereas; Romans 6 says the Jesus was made sin in order to create a setanic and perverse religion of Christianity. Read the Metu Netu Vol 2. - page 169. In Romans 6 this means that he was made disease prone, a murderer, a liar and a thief. Not only that! This is common sense. The fallacies of western religion, racism and culture has blinded the eys of many as they are of the sahu spirit. Their lower beings have been entangled into the web and net of the harlot of Ecc 7:26. Whereas; countless individuals have become heartless and immune to this form of setanic doctrine in order to fulfill their profane lust towards the cleverness of intellectualism and facism.

The food of the west will has been utilize to eliminate. Whereas; It's holy days become present on or during times of solstice's / full and new moons according to universal laws of God. All are of which the Bible and Quran forbids. They consider this paganism and polytheism. In addition; It's federal holidays (banking days) etc, too have been ordained in order to fulfill the european ancestry. However; they have banned African World Festival in some major cities as this includes = the celebration of Rev. Dr. Martin Luther King Jr. holiday - which fells during Lent! Moreover; this has inprisoned the male species of the African origin. Finally, the dietary laws of the Egyptian is filled with discipline and strict that Collosae 2:16-18 is denouncing the culture of the Africans of Ancient Khamit, Palestine and Canaan. This also includes the entire spectrum and ancestry towards the modernity of the origin of the African American.

The origin of the male species has been transformed into the female species due to the lack and therof; (single female) parenting system and the Christian revolution. This of which is the "holier than now" revolution. In this revolution there are hidden causatives throughout

3

the LGBT Movement. Whereas; there is no form of constructive discipline. However; the male child is often rewarded with follies of this modernized, egotistic and deformed democracy of which we currently reside.

You see, the western civilization has been determined to extinct and exterminate the Afro-American and the male prior to its its construction and reconstruction. In this; there has been the introduction of biochemical gasses that has been used in military missions. That is to say, by the Jews, Britons, Russians, Germans, Polish and people the Carribeans, South America and Asia. Indeed, the atrazine chemical, alcoholic beverages, heroin, crack-cocaine and marijuana has also been introduced as the quick high and the slow-kill syndrome. This also includes dairy and meat products. Such as pork and poultry.

Yes, they're manufactured and imported from overseas. Overseas, which includes The Asia Minor and Europe nations. The Europeans were inhabitants of the {Caucas Mountain Region} Whereas; the above listed are poisonous devices that will and has caused neurological disorders such as; Bipolar, Schitzophrenia, PSTD, ADHD, Parkinson's, Dementia, Alheimer's as well as other medical and mental disorders throughout the environment.

Those disorders are within Axis III and IV of the DSM. Indeed, this includes effiminization. Effiminization is when a man has shown typical characteristics of a female. This is also where hormones and chromosomes are misguided and misdirected by too much or a lack of estrogen (testosterone). X and Y chromosomes are disoriented by negative interactions within the dopamine inhibitors and the SSRI's (Selective Serotonin Reuptake Inhibitors).

In some cases pelvic inflammatory disease is caused by damaged to the urethra and ovaries. This is not due to STDS or other congenital factors and or disorders. Therefore; through chi gong, which is the healing of Ra life force with a beneficial dietary and health lifestyle will ensure longevity of an individual's lifespan. However; due to the epidemics of the AIDS virus, HIV virus, HPV virus and all forms of Hepatitis: All of the listed are pathogens that are due to the LGBT Movement, Alcoholism and drug addiction.

Therefore; effiminization of the male can be and is in most cases, situational. Whereas; the male child tends to spend the majority of his time around women - single women - (single parenting). Therefore; single women are heads of their own household and are filled with sexual perversions. They play both roles (man and woman) (trans sexualism) and or (Gender Disporia). Which are forms of mental illness. You see, in Africa, our ancestors who were women, were queens who were married to their male mate through spirituality not religious affairs. However; through colonialism and slave trade we as a people have been misinformed by and through western philosophy and education. We've been blackmailed and brainwashed through hypocrisy and greed.

Back to my point. The majority of them have multiple children by multiple deadbeat fathers who have been systematically enslaved as a result of a buraeucratic system that has been established not for the benefit of the so-called minority. The minority is the Black male. The Black Male has been brutalized through Islam, Christianity, Judaism and Catholic Church. Individuals - African and African American leaders such as Malcolm X, Nelson Mandela, Muhammad Ali, Marcus Garvey and others.

You see; The Bible, Canon and Quran weren"t written for the benefit of all people. That is to say, Africans and African American people. The theological books denounce African ancestry, oracles as well as spiritual divination. For they, themselves are children of a curse as a result of their hypocrisy and use of them themselves. For: their scriptures are of racism, hatred and discrimination as a result of causes of extremism. This is Islam, Christianity and Judaism.

The Black male has been conditioned to behave shamefully and lustfully and live the westernized lifestyle. Whereas; the Black man has shamed his own race by following anything with the lower part of his being and persuading others who are similar to his mishaps and follies of darkness. This is the mammilian aspects of the brain. You see, this is exactly what the western man and western culture has lived and taught within a culture of "anything goes" and where everything has been legalized by setiens of cleverness. This is the scheme of mankind. Man has conditioned himself into believing that he's always correct in his indecent proposals and seductions of immoralities through the double standards of living.

Double standards of living means that individuals seem to assume that they can have it both and all ways. Therefore; you cannot have it both ways. Blame the European, Jewish and Arab explorer and conqueror for those idolatrous and triggered behavioral patterns. You see, these negative triggered behavioral patterns are the reptillian _hippocampus) portion of the brain. In this; the cerebellum and the cerebral cortex become destablized due to constant negative pathological behavioral patterns of ideation and delusion. This is the result and conclusion of an individual's arrogance and highly esteemed methods of sensitivity due to its conditioned patterns of self-overindulging acts of pleasurable lusts.

This is with regards to the use of esteemed methods and fabricated conclusions (lies) by a variety of Egyptologist, psychoanalylistic scientist, educators and western renoun scholars of neurology, numerology, astrology, Christianity, LDS, Catholisim, Judaism and Islam. This also includes several Ausarians. You see, everything has been twisted. The lower being of individuals have and will always be diluted by those who invented slavery, ostracism and racism. This is to say'- earthly laws by mankind will never be capable of deharmonizing the universal laws that have been established by the Creator!

The SSRI's - Selective Serotonin Reuptake Inhibitors as well as the Dopamine inhibitors work together to form resonance within the brain to harmonize the life-force of (an) individual(s)! Energy is the movement of creation. Creation is the lif-force of creation and evolution. Evolution has been attempted by traditions (behavioralists) in order to secure their continue their reign over the ancient ancestry of the people of Kemet / Canaan and the African - Black Man.

However; through western religion = (unification) - we've been bamboozled by rhetoric and psychological systems of reward and discipline which are defined as to obey rules of behavior or suffer the consequence of punishment. You see; to correct an individual's behavior - the individual must recognize that there are problem(s)! Must recognize the problem(s). Then deal with his own problems of conditioned and negative - intolerable patterned behavior(s).

This is done through a ritualistic foundation of true spirituality. However; the societle norm of modernity has carnally whipped, shaped and psychologically manhandled us through its Watchtowers, Bibles, Quads, Qurans and Gay methods of the Tarot fortune-telling tactics. This is to transform the male through effiminization processes of transgenderizational patterns of EDUCATION-INFORMATION, GREED, DENIAL, LIES, HYPOCRISY & GAY PRIDE!

Within this; the systems of the world has hidden and denied the true ancestry of Kemet, Palestine and Canaan. Romans 1:25 mentions itself "who turned truth into a lie"! Rome and Greece are Caucausiod cultures that is and has been filled with deceit - greed, untamed lusts, shameless disease and filth. Those filthy lies have been told throughout the post ancient culture. In this; the need for mass incarceration, which is another form of behavioral punishment has been established in order to depopulate the black male by reinstitutionalizing his spiritual vessel.

The spiritual vessel has been restructured and reconditioned through schemes of the sublime. Influences of darkness and a variety of lustful enticements of pleasure has enslaved the black mind. These are of monetary value. Not to mention the fact that the second amendment has been violated by the constant providing of guns, alcohol and other forms of abusive drugs such as narcotics that are illegal. Whereas; it is the government that has provided the opportunities such as those to economically disadvantaged communities that are minority filled.

Mass destruction has come upon the Black Male in many forms. Self-Destruction has come upon the Black Male in many forms. This will never end as long as there are money-hungry clergymen and politicians who reign over one's lower being. Meaning weaknesses are monitored by the ministry. They seduce you into believing their religious dogma. In the meantime, they're obstructing your blessings while they are claiming and stealing your possessions.

In this; this is exactly why both the Holy Bible and Holy Quran were written. They were written in order to seduce the physiologically and psychologically lost in order to keep them in poverty and dictate them spiritually, emotionally, mentally and economically. Whereas; atrazine is an endocrine disrupter which is a persicide that is used in cleaning solutions as well as drinking water. It induces partial feminization in various living organisms.

You see, if you have read any of my writings you may already know where I am going with this. Atrazine is an Endocrine disrupter that causes genital tumors, cancers, learning disabilities, ADHD and other forms of psychiatric and anxiety disorders. This therefore, causes dopamine inhibitors and SSRI's to become dysfunctional. Dopamine inhibitors act as neurotransmitters and coicide with tyrosine that is already within the brain. This controls moods and other behavioral patterns of mental and spiritual disturbance.

However: in many cases. In all cases, behaviors are conditioned both objectively and subjectively. They are conditioned by lack, need, want, desire, pleasure and more. This is to say - that the interior of the brain contains various houses. These houses work together and independently to assist living organisms in their capacity to manifest and live according to whatever their desires are or whatever needs must be fulfilled in their lives of mental and spiritual evolution.

Therefore; the brain can be disrupted, harmed and disabled by the following; inflammation, lack of oxygen, other fluids and or disabled blood cells. In many cases; man has caused his own problems. However; through slavery, mental slavery, lies and brainwashing, it is my conclusion that a fool will believe anything. A fool will do anything. A fool will fool himself.

In addition; intermingling has caused this huge turnout of terror, hatred and racism. In this; race relations with atrazine, effiminization and the Black Man - has actually failed the Black Male by the means of him turning on his own race and mating with the european mistress / converting to LDS / Christianity / Islam / Judaism and etc.

If a black man has studied any form of religious and histological teachings, he'd understand the lack of God within them. Therefore; a fool teaches what he lacks. All of which are lies. Therefore; the Black Male has been effiminized through self-overindulgings of chemical and mental genocidal behaviors due to the lack of the understanding his own ancestry as well as lacking the understanding of the the true Ausarian / Canaanite & Palestinean.

In most cases; his mental and phycical incarceration can be due to substance induced mood disorders as well as histrionic and narcisstic disorders. In these disorders, individuals speak boldly and proudly of their intelligence of (Islam-Black History and racial issues) which they've acquired while incarcerated as result of being in isolation leading to addiction to substances and criminal activity. They are manipulative just as the slave owners of which they put down through conversations of delusion and granduer. In this, they are sly and quick thinking schemers as are their criminal ancestors were throughout ancient and world history to modernity.

In modernity, intercessors are used by western ministry on behalf of others. Now, this can be effiminization, bigotry and idolatry for many purposes. Deuteronomy 28:29 mentions that you will grope at noon and no one will save you. Philipians 2:12 says work out you own salvation! So what's the point? The point that i am trying to make is the following; You see, religion means to unite - bring unity amongst all people. However; in this, it sanctions African divination - spiritual powers that are equal to the universal laws which governs daily events.

In addition; western religion and theology has often misunderstood its own lack of knowledge and understanding to the point of communism, racism and massacres that have been devoted to the demoralization of particular groups of people. Whether it is due to the fact that it is due to ethnicity and or sexual orientation. Indeed; the Bible tell us that man was created in the image and likeness of God. However; man has been misguided and seduced by his own misunderstandings. God, therefore, forbids acts of the LGBT and perverse methodologies (self-less behaviors)!

9

Also, note; The Holy Quran is also infoms us in Surah 17:75-77 that individuals will be doomed while they are alive, prior to death, during death and after death. Therefore; for many reasons, intercessing on another individual's behalf can be harmful to everyone involved.

Back to the point of Deuteronomy 28:29; which mentions that no one will save you. Is this and can this be true. You cannot have it both ways. Individuals, Mankind and That Black Male has committed acts of vile (sin) in knowing that it is wrong! Philipians 2:12 says 'work out your own salvation with fear and trembling'. Therefore; you have fallen from your own arrogance {grace}! You are fooling yourselves! Therefore; you have become hopeless and in self-denial as to having (MDD) Major Depressive Disorder.

In addition; you rome from brownstone to brownstone - church to church due to your own insecurities and egotistical values and ways. This is due to your rememberance of biblical verses. Verses; that forbid to provide cure for your self-inflicted impurities -{Deuteronomy 28:61} because of your Christo-Islamic and Judeao schemes of hypocrisy.

Therefore; intercession has been manipulated by the western civilization in order to fulfill its needs of desire and greed. In this, the effiminate male with assistance from the mosque, temple and church has chosen secret - un-hidden manipulation methods of the weak and lowly as a means of easing his own internal disorders. Man then turns to methods of superstitional tarot, horoscopes and daily devotionals. All of which has no spiritual base - of working out his salvation.

This doesn't work! You see, with the politics of special education and prison systems in their attempt to reform the Black male into depopulation as well as effiminization, the western civilization has failed into its own chastisement. The unknown writer of the book of Hebrews mentions in Hebrews 12:8 the following; But if ye be without chastisement, wherefore; we are all partakers, then are ye Bastards and not sons! We have been bastardized by a country of slavers who raped, maimed, mutilated and murdered the African ancestry. Whereas; the United States Constitution and Holy Bible were written by the white man. They've castrated, debated and formed Jim Crowism through ostracizing social and spiritual nations with what they and considered acts of God!

Self-chastisement comes from the creator dwelling within each individual. The Tree of Life allows us to be a mirror image of God. In this; knowing what our individual strengths and weaknesses of the spirit are. However; it the word transgression is termed as an act or acts against the laws, rules and the will of God! This includes societal norm(s)? Therefore; Isaiah 53:5 mentions that he (the Lord) was bruised for our transgressions and wounded for our iniquities. You see, this was the Judaeo form that led to the excuse and rise of Christianity. Whereas; amongst the Ten Commandments it says otherwise: {THOU SHALT NOT KILL}!

You see; the entire Holy Bible is contrary to its every allegorical fashion of idolatry. In other words, Its words were written by faggots and bigots. I also have a problem with the Holy Quran. The Surah / - The Holy Quran and the hypocrisy of Prophet Mohammed has done more harm to the black mans spirit, character and personality. Surah 17:75-76 death shall come upon all none believers through Allah's Judgement due to their blindness and failure to obey its teachings!

Deuteronomy 13:5 This is where false prophets are to be killed. However; it says "Thou Shalt not kill"! Do you get my point. Good. This has caused the Black man to murder his brethren, steal from his brethren, deny his brethren, lie to and about his brethren. This has also caused the Black man to have effiminizing relations with his brethren. Romans 1 mentions this. However; its author was identified as a murderer, deceiver and mocker of God! We are living in a world that has been rehaped and reconstructed by a web of fallacies of fabrication.

The caucasian has deceived the Black Man and the Black Man has turned on his own race and ancestry due to his unstable mind and il-hearted behavior manifestations. You see, after forms of systemic discrimination the black man has in many cases been deceived by his own hypocrisy and has eventually turned into his own vomit. Deception has been on the mind of the European since their forefathers constant invasians and reconstructions of the United State of America.

11

As many of us may have known, the America's have been here thousands of years prior to it being recognized by settlers, cannibals and conquerors who had colonized its natives with sinful and torturous activities that are and were inhumane acts against God. You see, In the beginning was the Word and the Word was with God. However; that was written by the Arab, Jew and Christianizing Papacy during the fourteenth century in order of the continuance and the distribution of chattel slavery throughout the Atlantic and Middle Passage.

Slavery and effiminization of the Black Male is also spiritual and psychological. Conditioned behavioral patterns are disharmonizing towards one's spirit. Personalities and characteristics can disharmonized the entire brain as well DNA and RNA of th Xh homosexual producing gene that is within the female. Heterozygous females and the neuroanatomy of homosexuality as a result of hypothalamus disorders and immature nervous system! Sexual Dimorphism within the anterior commisure that can be a result of hypothalamo-pituitary disorders and dysfunctions due to cancerous viruses within them.

Chemical Castration

Chemical Castration is when there is a use of prescribed medications along with street drugs that eventually cause individuals to have low libido, Hypothalamus, pituitary gland disorders and diseases. Meaning; there becomes a lack of interest in intimacy as a result of a low sex drive. These prescribed medications are as follows;

A. Depakote

B. Doxapin

C. Theothoxine

D. Depakane

E. Navane

F. Medroxyprogesterone Acetate

The listed are also used in and as antipsychotic, anti-manics and antidepressants in veterinary medicine. Note: Chemicals are compounds of substances that eventually create a {substance} in the form of a liquid, powder or pill! In addition; in psychiatry as well as within animal toxicology, Medroxyprogesterone Acetate has been used to castrate sex-offenders and child molesters of pedophilia. You see, this particular medication has also been used for transgendered and bisexual males. Whereas; this is after slavers created sex farms that enhanced the effiminization of the black male during slavery and during this period of modernity incarceration. Slavery and incarceration of black male youth and adults are at all time highs

Court-ordered psychiatry, paychiatry triggers mental instabilities along with homosexual and transgendered tendencies of the black male due to the prescribing of psychotropics. The triggers of homosexuality and STD's of HPV, HIV and AIDS can also be assessed through hypnosis within the lines of psychotherapy and certain practices of divination within the church, mosque or temple. This also includes gay-witchcraft and gay-tarot. This is of which the student fails to seek council from an elder or sheperd. However; in many cases; the elders of the ministry are utilizing this deadly craft as they continue to sacrifice their members by using bible verses to continue to justify and distribute idolatrous harm upon others in this society of behavioral and conditioned patterns of lust.

That is how they gain followers: 2 Peter 2:14 they are unstable souls and which are prone to psychiatric problems and or sudden changes of behavior / mood. Homosexuals whereas; 2Peter 2:22 The dog returns to his own vomit. In the majority of biblical scripture, dog is a representation of homosexual. You see; The European Union and effiminizational gayisms are coupled with The WHO - World Health Orginization's improper dealings with uses of vaccinations and prescription medications that have been altered and altered pregnancies and lactations of women and their fetus. Whereas; many prescribed medications often trigger prenatal disabilities as well as anomalies within the lives of many.

In many ways, injections with syringes have infected individuals with various STD's and pneumonias. In this; these are acts of genocide by WHO - The World Health Organization throughout the world. This has gone on throughout the world - [especially Third World countries] where poverty and starvation occurs. In many cases; this is like a Influenza and Zika. However; different due to the causes of ADHD, MDD, Schizophrenia, Bipolar Disorder and other forms of life-long brain damaging pathogens of mental illness and confusion.

In this; there are personality disorders that are undiagnosed towards the Black Male. This therefore; has led to mass murders, mass shootings, so-called race riots and the inhumane epidemics of transvestism and transexualism. This has been a pattern of the LGBT movement by the European throughout their conquests of many nations prior to Yeshua, Christ and Mohammed being born and represented as spiritual leaders according to western religions that are of Jewish, Catholicism, LDS, Christian and Muslim sects.

They have disuaded the African male from the Paut Neteru method and replaced it with the PTSD forms of westernizational paganism as well as setianism. This is with westernized methods of metaphysics and philosophy. This is where individuals study and learn about Greek philisophers. However; they are unlearned regarding the lifestyles of those philosophers what and where those philosophers gained their knowledge. Indeed; it was ancient Egypt (Khamit). In addition; in Greco-Romantism; the Oracle of Delphi / Phythia was used by the priestess and Clement of Alexandria. Individuals assummed that this was the nature of polytheistic Egyptians who worshipped several pagan gods during the hellenistic periods of the ancient Greco-Roman Empires. Egypt has always been montheistic. This is contrary to the Bible and statements by countless Egyptologists.

Back to my point. You see; It has been reported the The United States of America's population is 13% of African decent. While on the otherhand, 40 - 50% of them are enslaved by incarceration. Who knows what percentage of us have been murdered. What percentage of us have been murdered by police officers as well as due to white on Black Crime and why. Personality disorders occur due to individuals lacking knowledge of themselves. However; through african spirituality - Eastern Culture - of the Paut Neteru which consists of seven personalities via characteristics of God. This is contrawise in western religion, philosophy and culture where there are aspects of the so-called holy Trinity. In this; there is a belief and imagination of false, fictitious forms of hope through a form of faith through their followers having no proof of a life - burial (tomb) of their saviour. This too holds true in Islam.

In addition; the male has been castrated with enchanted and invoked methods of mourning by intercessory and European military tactics of the ancient Judeao-Greco-Roman theological and philosophical method.

Galatians 1: 13-14. This is of the ritualized and cannabilized methods according to Lamentations 2:20 and throughout the Bible. Shall the women eat their fruit of a span long! This of which also includes Acts 15:29 as far as abstaining for meats / foods sacrificed to idols. Whereas; Jesus allowed demons to enter pigs in Matthew 8: 28-34 after they asked to be saved by entering the swine

Therefore; why westerners, would you eat that of which what has been so-called demonized with demons according to your foreknowledge of STD's, obesity, liver disease, diabetes, anxiety and heart disease. In addition; an abyss is a dark and deep chasm. Therefore; demons were in the chasm. A chasm is a separation due to a code of conduct of which is of the abyss is spoken of in Lk 8:31. Throughout Judaism, it is within their doctrine that they {not eat swine}: It is and was forbidden. Contrawise to Jesus' declaration that all foods are clean throughout the following verses in Mark 7:14-23.

These personalities of the swine / wild boar are then triggered into the mind of the Male. This then tends to cause pathological illnesses that can be triggered perversly. These illnesses include the following; blood disorders, tumors, brain and behavioral disorders that are due to extreme forms of emotional overindulgence relating to perversions throughout the thought process. This is where the thought process becomes ignited by sublimes, delusions and grandious methods of disoriented of schemes of ideation. In psychiatry, this is considered mania.

Moving right along! This is also due to the United States of America's Food and Drug Administration's falure to take action as it has allowed and prevailed in committing intentional homocide by creating and poisoning foods. In most cases individuals were fed rats unknowingly. These foods also include the following; Dairy products, poultry and fish products. Whereas; animals have been injected in order of financial gain. Those foods tend to cause a variety of health issues even death to millions of unkowldgable individuals. This is contrary to Collosae 2:16. In addition; throughout slavery, we were, our ancestory were fed off our own peers and tissues that were useless towards the slaver. We too were the sodomized on slave farms as exibitions of exploitation. Males then became prostitutes as well as homosexuals.

In addition; this activity still exists to this day! Men and women of color have been enshrined into mental slavery as they have sought glamour, fame and ways of living beyond their financial means. This is shameful whereas, we must have a holistic culture that is spirited with moral forms of civility.

Blind Psychiatry The Myth of Born in Sin Vs. The Paut Neteru's 7 Personalities

LINKAGE THAT RESIDES WITH SEVERAL PRIOR EGYPTIAN DYNASTIES

Sin is violation of the will of the creator that is unknowingly within you. There's a divine plan that is within each person according to the Will that is within each individual that has been provided (given) by the Creator - god that is within each individual. Sin is due to individuals having over-indulging emotions that are triggered by patterns of emotional instability. Therefore; what if your god / saviour or prophet was of the Ausarian Culrure? Would you worship the same or worship that individual god. Would you then be a hypocrate regarding your so-called religion, whether it is one of the following;

Catholicism

Taoism

Bhuddism

Confucianism

Christianity

SDA

Jehovah's Witness

Canon

Gnosticism

Judaism

LDS

Rastafarianism

Islam

Orthodox Judeao - Greco-Roman Theology

LGBT

Catholic - Lutheran Church

Bahaism

Shamanism

Aren't Eastern religions and cultures forbidden throughout The Holy Quran, Bible and Quad. You see; sin was formed to create fear in the hearts and minds of individuals. Has anyone of you heard of the Zero dynasty!

Moving right along! The Bible mentions that God has not given us the spirit of fear but of a sound mind and might. You see; sin occurs within ones person, spirit and characteristics due to the overindulgence of emotions of externalized activities that are controlled by untamed mechanisms of perception, thought and hasty forms imaginational delusion.

Whereas; Jeremiah 23 and Roman 3:4 are similar and contrary towards each other. As they are the Old and New Testaments. As every man is a liar. This is where individuals create forms of self-delusion within their minds as their egos rise like orgasms. They are self-proclaimed Bishops-Ministers-Apostoles and Prophets. This is where the African ancestry has been lost towards and as a result of westernized methods of religion and philosophies of savagry, education and slavery.

Individuals were continually are currently disuaded within themselves from the ancestry of the Zero Dynasty- Palestine -Kemet - and Canaan while being enslaved into the ravagry of westernized forms and methodologies of Arabizational and Christianizing religions of sacred hatreds. The Bible and Quran are too similar in their allegorical methods and methods of indoctornal brainwashing. Their spiritual leader are like minor Charles Mansons. Whereas; Numbers 13: Canaan was constantly explored and spied on as directives of Their Ruler/Lord in response to the people's request.

In contrast; Galatians 2:4 They spied out our liberty in Christ Jesus. Therefore; Christianity, Islam and other western religions are allegorical and imaginary in their philosophical philosophies. You see; western religion is delusional upon the Black - Male. It lacks substance. This means that it seeks a god outside of one's self. I by no means mean self-rightcheousness and arrogance. He who seeks which is within will find the kingdom of God! Therefore; too 2 Corinthians 5:21 He was made Sin by Christianity's use of the ancient Judeao-Greco-Roman theological and biblical concepts of crucifixion that was created and based on the fact that ancient Kemet was the sole originator and provider of sound doctrine of a monotheistic rite.

Also; it mentions in the Old Testament in various passages that no one and nothing is to be sacrificed. This is to idols. This is murder. Murder due to arrogance. Everything living creature created is created by a male and female. (Yin-Yang) The two are not alike. They are unified and glorified as one in their creation of a son / man-child!

You see, the people of Gaul and Corinth practiced animism and druids -human sacrificed millions. They were dignitaries and were worshipping Celtic Belgiumic animals and pagan forms of wood. The boar was highly worshipped as well as Dis Patar by the Romans as well!

Finally, explore means to travel in an unfamiliar territory and become familiar with its people and customs in order to conquer it by mingling and later destroying it greatness. It's greatness of the Male as the GLBT has never been a part of the eastern civilization. Especially, ancient Khamit, Palestine and Canaan. It is the western thought that has astranized the Black Male and the African Culture.

Romans 6 says "he was made sin". Who in their right mind would make someone constantly commit sinful acts. In addition; no creature, no living organism is born without a cell of sperm or ovary. Therefore; who made him (Jesus) commit sin? The story was stolen from Kamit's story of Ausar! Metu Neter V. I page220 mentions the fact that man cannot save himself from the mere employment of his Will. Phillipians 2:12 mentions that man is to work out his own salvation with fear and trembling. However: if God hasn't not given us the spirit of fear but he has given us a sound mind and might - / we therefore; have the Paut Neteru. The Paut Neteru is 7 personalities and characteristics of God.

Therefore; Blind psychiatry and western religion has plagarized Kamit, Palestine and Canaan and shamed them by creating Judaism, Christianity and Islam. You are then persecuted de to your knowledge and lifestyle of the ancients.

Psychiatry is geared towards the healing of various mental, mood and behavioral disorders. However; this becomes racially bias by the practitioner. Psychiatry's history was so-called created by Professor Johann Christian Reil of Halle, Germany in 1808. This occurred during, prior to and after the Hatian Revolutionary war of 1804. This additionaly impacted the institution of slavery and the revolution of St. Domonigue during the French Revolution within the Caribbean culture. Note; The Moors, Caribs and Arwawaks of West Africa and Spain were also victims of Christopher Columbus unlawful deeds of greed and bigotry. Columbus met them in his travels towards cannibalism and racial bigotry towards the indigenous African Race. In this; the religion of Santeria / Orisha were converted unto the Catholicism. Whereas; the church had gotten its rites from ancient Egypt.

In addition; The Garifuna tribe / people of honduras, the Caribbean and Africa were auctioned and sent into chattel slavery. As a result, they too were enriched and induced into criminal activity, poverty, racial tensions and cannibalism. In this; psychiatry within the pulpit of the Christian Church and Jewish Synagogues had risen to exceeding levels. The setien blinds the eyes of the lowly by bewitching them and tormenting their lower being. Whereas; individuals were and are victims of messages of a savior outside of themselves through brainwashing techniques of psychological and institutional modifying techiniques of westernizing philosophical forms of rhetoric.

Indeed it's rhetoric. You see, Romans 1:30 man has created evil things that controls and brainwashes others by attacking their weaknesses. On the otherhand; The Kamitic Tree of Life arouses one's soul, mind, spirit and being. Whereas; we judge ourselves, behavioral conditions, pattens by allowing us towards self-resurrection, self reconciliation and restoration / self-restoration. You see, the Bible talks grace as it mentions that we are not of ourselves - lest any man shall boast. Ephesians 2:8-9 (Ephesus) was also within Ancient Greece and the Asia Minor! This is where the seed of philosophicals that had been planted, formed and tranformed into to the mind and spirit of the African civilization. They are using television actors, entertainers, sports figures and sitcoms to seduce you into a web of hypocrisy, deceit and lies.

In modernity, restoration means that the seed has to be restored to its original existence. Therefore; origin and chosen are two different words which has different definitions and purposes. As you should know by now, information does not improve an individuals behavior. It is the the guidance of ancestry, proper diet, rest and health through meditation / exercise etc!

In addition; psychaitrical Rosicrucian Cabalism is the path to destruction. Whereas; it along with Greece's form of philosophy and christendom has destablized the Black race with mindboggling untruths and forms of Arabizing through the Arab slave trade. Throughout the Arab slave trade, children were sold as exploitational sex slaves and murdered while the men of Africa, Persia, The South Sudan, Egypt and the West Indes were castrated. In this; indeed, the 7th century AD was the Islamic Slave Trade proved to have consisted of over more than 150 million individuals.

This is an epigenetic form of systemic racism and bigotry of created by Judaism, Christendon and Islam. Surah 23:12-14 Man we created from a quintessence of clay, a clot of spern of congealed blood of pure substance. Either is the meaning of quintessenced racism in those verses. Genesis 3:19 and 2:27 You were made from dust and will leave theis earth in dust. We have all of the periodic elements within us.

Switching gears unto pharmas as forms of psychiatric medicines and chemicals that have become addictive. Whereas; the White race has become abusive and violent in order to receive them. In addition; all psychiatric drugs such as the listed cause impotence, prostatitis, urinary tract infection, hepatitis and liver cirrhosis according to The Physicians Desk Reference volume 67 pg. (2641). This is where it disusses the many stipulations of Abilify. on the otherhand; Navane, which is another psychotropic medication produces the same result. This is written in Volume 50 of the Physicians Desk Reference on pg. (2201) For mood disorders, manic episodes, MDD, Bipolar and Schizophrenia.

You see; eastern religion and spiritual cultivation is unlike western theocracy of Arabizing the Black race. The Paut Neteru is a heavenly host of evidential facts that reveals that man has a multiplicity of manifestations of the image of God! Psychiatry, on the otherhand, is aware of the capacity of the right brain. That is to say the Carl Jung and {Bisexual} Aliester Crowley has failed the Black race due to their denial as they have used Rosicrucian Psychiatrical Cabalism to manipulate the manipulating Egyptologists into denying the minds of the people of kamit with forms of complex psychiatry, analytical psychiatry and behavioral instincts.

Therefore; man is incomplete. Whereas; mankind hasn't fulfilled itself due to his / her conditions and patterns of depersonalization. Depersonalization deals with individual manipulation. In this, there comes a time as well as times when individuals must recognize that man {he-she}cannot save itself from overindulging patterns of hallucination, negative perverse fantasy, negative perverse desire and negative perverse imagination. This is through the overpowering indulgence of conditioned emotional patterns that are externalizing factors and uncontrolling forms of anxieties, lusts and anger. This produces negative behavioral and thought patterns of delusion and granduer.

These patterns of behavior tend to become a sheild of unproductable stimuli - the lack thereof of Geb. Geb, which is the life-force of mans indwelling intelligence as well as his entire anatomical anatomy. This is internal as well as external. The enternal man then becomes the outward. In a sense; there is a form of balance verses inbalance infrastructure within the self and person.

How many times have you done something when you knew that it wasn't the right thing to do. How many spiritual laws have you violated unknowingly verses knowing. And Vice versa. What is man! Psalms 8 and Genesis 6 are compelling and contrawise. In one sense, David is praising Gods works of creating and on the otherhand; it mentions the anger of God of his own works. Numbers 23:19 God is not a man that he shall lie; neither is he the son of man that he shall repent. The reader has been bewitched. Galations 3:1 Oh foolish Galatians who bewitched you? Whereas; you have refused to use your spiritual perception. Galatians 3:10 cursed is everyone who does not continue to do what is and has been written in the book of the law.

Timothy 1:8-10 says: The law is good if one uses them and it properly. Moreover; the laws of the universe and God are correlations within each other. The law is the Tree of Life verses the polytheistic methodology of Hebraic Cabalism. In addition; the Kemetic Tree of Life governs The spiritual law(s) that govern the seasons, times and cycles as well as sequences and changes of the solar system and patterns of the moon. This then becomes ritualized within a spiritual culture of the people of ancient Palestine, Canaan-Judah and Kemet. All of which is forbidden within the Holy Bible and the Quran. For the two consider this paganism, idolatry and polytheism.

This is a huge misconception regarding mainstream religions and psychiatrical screening. This is also considered a religious and or spiritual problem which relates to forms of graduer and or delusion according to all of the psychiatrical forms within Axis diagnosing of particular behavioral scaling. Whereas; this is the claim of the psychiatrist / clergy as mental forms of the destablization of humanity, maining the people of color. This is written in the DSM Volume 5 of the 2012 Diagnostic Code V62.89. Psychiatrist consider mental illnesses concurrent with an individuals religious or spiritual lifestyle.

In addition; information does not improve conditioned behaviors and spiritual infirmities. It only hinders an individuals progression towards healing. Spiritual infirmities occur due to an individial's inability to understand the differences between being informed, understanding and knowing. Numbers 23:9 is a representation of God so-called sayings of; to be informing the people that they do not know themselves. Whereas; the people have continued to sin to a degree of unhealthiness regarding poor health decisions and using poverty as excuses for tormoil within their lives. They have then turned unto all forms of idolatrous behavioral patterns of madness.

Hosea 4:6 My people are destroyed because a lack of knowledge; because thou has rejected knowledge. This has lead to the emasculation of the male as well as lesbianism of the female and progression of the LGBT Movement. Indeed; immorality has to be confronted by the clergy, practitioner as well as the client.

Matthew: 10:34 I come not to bring peace but the sword. This is contrary to Job 26:10 where it says {follow peace with all men} Jesus also mentions; "I have come to bring man against his father, daughter against mother". "A man's enemies will be of his own household"! You see; psychiatry and clergy has whipped individuals with seducing spirits {familiar spirits} of Judeao-Greco-Romantistic methodologies of vain philosophies. Those philosophies have entangled the blind into the netted web within the western civilization. This is also within in Ecc 7:6-10 as a form of greed, slavery and racisms. Individuals have become immune to the various forms of entanglement and self-entrapment. The sword is a symbol of the seal of The United States of America as well as The American Psychiatric Association.

In this; man turns against his father by committed acts of homosexuality. 1 Corinthians 6:9 and Romans 1:24. Women as well in turning from the guidance of the mother and began whoring: In addition; there were and throughout modernity, there are male shrine prostitutes who were and are detestable as they're ancestors were the captors of Canaan. This was practiced this in 1 kings 14:24. The captors were of European ancestry. For those reasons they have twisted the history of The African people. Psalms 56:5 as long as they twist my words and all of their schemes are for my ruin. Whereas Exodus 23:8 Do not accept a bribe. A bribe blinds those who see and twists the words of the innocent.

Therefore; slavery is not good! Mental slavery is not good. In addition perception is to see, feel and hear something through the senses. Therefore; who did you allow to bewitch your SSRI's. Who has secretly bewitched your SSRI's? Whereas; clergymen will destablize an individual(s) by infecting their entire brain formation by inducing them with patterns of psychiatrical and deforming behaviors, moods and appetites of uncleanliness.

Psychiatrists too have failed to find a consistent correlation between depressive illness and behavior personality type. This includes the type of particular psychodynamic mechanism. Whereas; studies have indicated that there has been a diminish to and of the importance of environmental factors in explaining all forms of depression and psychiatric disability. (pg) - 1334 {Principals of Neurology} 8th Edition!

Refer to the Metu Neter Vols 1-9 for the personalities of the Tree of Life! They will be refreshing to the mind, person, spirit and soul. This will enable you to be free from sickness, pain and anxieties that the world has to offer. The Tree of Life Meditation System is a system of healing conditions and behavioral patterns through meditation, Qi Gong and a healthy - nutritious vegan dietary lifestyle. This lifestyle will create a much greater way of living and immorality amongst the people of color.

In addition, one must go much deeper within self and studies in order of birthing true passionate wisdom as it relates to processes of intermingling and certain processes of transgenetic manipulation through biochemical and bio-organical sciences of neurological and psychiatrical studies in order of comprehending this book as well as the holistic truths of the origins of creation, sin, racism and hatred.

Sins Of Amerika Hades

Hades is the Greek god of the underworld.

Hell is a term that was created by mankind in order to manipulate the lower being of individuals and control them by inducing fear within their hearts about a fictional savior. In this, clergymen are negligent. They have become wealthy from blind recipients who are impoverished unstable and ignorant towards the facts regarding spirituality. Truly; they often preach grace. However; there is no grace at all. Grace is often used by tele-evangelists in order to soothe their congregations and their arrogant concious.

Leviticus 27:29 None devoted which shall be devoted unto to man shall be redeemed. For those who are doomed are not redeemed. Devoted is to be loyal, true, steadfast and lovable. In this; in ancient Khamit Auset was devoted unto Ausar who was maimed into 14 pieces and murdered by his brother Set. You see, Set is also know as the judicial and political system of which we the people have been carnalized by. There is a scheme of the setien to continue to shame his family as written in parables of Matthew 10:34-36 with regards to "I am coming with the sword"!

Ezekiel 39:1-29 I am coming at you Gog. Gog was the son of Japheth, Japheth was the son of Noah. Gog-Magog were of the caucasian race. Alexander the Greats [Greek) tribesmen who envaded ancient Syria and Palestine were persistent in theirquest for the primative lands of Egypt and Canaan. In this; Jeremian 51:27 is where Askenaz - the {Scythians} who were the Zoroastrians - {Pre-Islam-Israelites} were one of the people and nations who were chosen to disdain Russian and Prussian war groups. This was prophesied by Jeremiah. There is also a mention of the finale of the old world and the becoming of the new world order.

You see, Gomer / was the father of the Scythians. Gomer too was of Japheth. The Scythians were of the Turkish Iranians. Obadiah 1:20 They were warful and a people of aggression. They were fighting for Canaan and Palestine. However; it is never mentioned in modernity. Whereas; Christianity is a setienistic doctrine which promotes greed, hatred, bigotry, racial violence and poverty wars of genocide. With this, Christianity also arabizes individuals with the twisted and perplexed schemes of conversion.

Job 10:21-22 Before I go to the place of no return, to the land of gloom and utter darkness, to the land of deepest night and utter darkness and disorder where even the light is like darkness. Ancient Mesopotamia - Canaan-Palestine-Kemet" have been considered Houses of darkness" by the Egyptologist, Caucasian, Arab, Israeli and authors of the old and testaments as well as the masonic Cabalists! Without the Devil - there's no Christianity nor Islam of the Greco-Romantic philosophy of metaphysical life forces. Those of which have manured upon the heads of the lowly.

You see; Job was suicidal while living in disarray as written earlier in 10:19. If only I had never come into being, or had been carried straight from the womb to the grave. No return means what to the reader of that particular verse - vain imagination! Genesis 6 says that god said that he had hated and disliked what he had created after man had commited sin. Numbers 23:19 God is not a human that he should change his mind and nother is he the son of man that he shall repent. I must ask whether or not the oracles were rephrased.

In addition; delusion and granduer are coupled with psychotic episodes which leads to one's own destruction. To utter is to chant during meditation in order of invocation as it relates to energies that an individual is attempting to manifest in order to shape - improve a form of condition or conditions that haven't been stilled.

You see; the Tree of Life of ancient Khamit allows man to seek within himself the vital signs of nutritrional healing. The meat of the spirit and integrity of the soul has to become balanced with a holistic attainment of achievable and realistic goals towards one in finding self. 1 Corinthians 3:2 I fed you with milk and meat and you could not bear it. Indeed: I use biblical passages in order to gain your understanding of its allegorical hipocrisies. For; it's intentions of the Holy Bible are for the clergy to use - {for its own benefit}. For those purposes, there is a failed economy, the wealthy remains wealthy and the blind have remained in states of vagabondage fallacy.

In addition; Ecc 9:10 whatever your hands find to do, do it well for the realm of the dead is where you are going. There is no planning, no knowledge nor wisdom. Therefore; you cannot make it to heaven based on a worldly resume of credentials. Revelations 20:12 The Books The dead were opened and individuals were judged for what they had done. This has been stolen from The spirituality of ancient Kemet, Palestine, Canaan and Judah, The Story of Ausar! Whereas; page 222. of the Metu Neter Vol. 1 mentions that the male aspects of Seker, which is controlled by the spiritual forces (Ptah) houses the conscious and will} of the deceased who failed to live in harmony with the laws of Maat- {divine laws} Timothy 1:10 and Galatians 3:13 Therefore; are you living a destiny of curse and misfortune. What are the spiritual forces that you are invoking.

For they ban sound doctrine 2 Timothy 4:3. In addition Every since Briton, France and America bombarded the peace treaty that was a misguided ventor of the purchasing of the State of Louisiana and various states by the United States of America from France in 1803, it has been total chaos along with a strong representation of racism, hatred and greed. In this; lies have filled the cranium, soul and spirit of the African and African American. Discussions and sermons have been given by false teachers, prophets, bishops evangelists and the orthodox. Lies have been told and the clergy has blindsided and robbed the Black community with lusts of hypocrisy, perversions and homosexuality of the LGBT Movement. This has been a grandious state of instability by ministeries, foreign ministers, presidents, supreme court justices, legislatures, members of the senate as well as members of congress.

Note: In this; Amelia Bassanno Lanier {Shakespeare's Dark Lady} wrote Shakespeare's plays and other works for him. Whereas; it is mentioned that Shakespeare translated the Bible. However; how can this be? Indeed! If Shakespeare couldn't read or write, of course, it had to be translated. Therefore; he was illiterate. In addition; racism is a dog to its teeth! In many cases, dog is a parable for LGBT in the Bible. Also, note; it is a representation for a male prostitute and or whoremonger - harlot. He, Shakespeare too was bisexual according to his twenty-six Dark Lady sonnets. Also; it has been said that The Holy Bible is the most popular book in The United States of America and the entire world!

Filled with hundreds of allegorical and inconsistencies statements and testimonial flaws. This is to say Mark 5:10-20 Why would you eat what was punished by Jesus. Whereas Jesus punished the swine and demons. Whereas; he later declared all foods clean in Mark 7:19 Food is a representation of love and charity along with wisdom. Those are parables. Food means Knowledge, Wealth, Prosperity, Wisdom and Understanding. Hebrews 6 Let us go into perfection by resurrecting the dead and leaving the elementry principles of Christ! Therefore; Surah 22:5 O' people are you in doubt about the Resurrection that you were created by us from dust, a germ, a clot and finally a lump of dust. In addition; resurrection means to awaken your godman spirit and arousal of Sakkara-Seker!

The United States of America along with Greece has stolen its symbolism from ancient Egypt, Palestine and Canaan. However; both the Khamitic and Canaanite views and ways of life have been sanctioned by biblical scholars, the European and the entire western civilization. Whereas; Hades has taken and shaped the affairs of all areas of humanity. Hades is a Greek god - known as positive regardless of its aspects of the underworld; Underworld is the otherworld thought that is the abyss and or beneath the surface of the world in most religions, cultures and mythodoligies. It also means she'ol, spirit and soul of a man. This of which is a place of darkness to which all the dead go. According to Judaism - The Hebrew Bible: This includes righteous and unrighteous irregardless of the choices they've made while they were alive.

On the otherhand; The United States of America has been demonized. Demonized by itself since its origin by its so-called founding fathers who used the teachings of Hades and serapis to translate humankind into into its ways of hatred, bigotry and racism. Whereas; Aboriginines existed first within this nation {America} prior to the enforced methods of arrogance and of greed!

In 1946, in his visit to Lincoln University in Pennslyvania, Albert Einstein mentioned (a) fact that racism is a disease of White People. In most cases; many are unaware of this. However; it has been inherited through geneology along with toxoplasmosis. Toxoplasmosis is a parasitic disorder that is within animal blood and feces as it then comes into contact with humans. Also, note; that beastiality plays a role in this as well. In this; the majority of individuals of the caucasoid race are privileged through their vile acts of affluenza disorders as a result of their indulging acts of arrogance and greed.

You see, America was created based upon the hidden origins and principals of Ancient Egypt / Canaan. Also, note; it was redeveloped on the basis of Judaism and Islam which finalized Americas sinful movements. Judaism and Islam assisted in the establishment of the Americas by invading, conquering and enslaving Africans within their African nations, cultures by disallowing them (us) to practice our cultural spirituality. This is of which has become shameful to many African Americans today.

In addition; according to Exodus 23:6 The world and The United States of America has perverted justice by multiplying and denying all races the Four Freedoms @ an equalistic approach. It has been a revolving door with regards to the idolatrous acts that were committed by the conquistadors, those who conquered the natives in America. This is where the Aboriginal people first resided. Whereas; they were Africans.

For; I will make you fishers of men. Matthew 4:19 and Mark 1:17. Whereas; he gave them nets and they followed him. The nets were to captivate (captives) slaves and to make them follow religious fallacies of hatred and bigotry through the brainwashing of the meager (fish) human beings. This is to treat them as lower class citizens. Does fisher of men reply to Ecc 7:26? Whereas; SLAVERY has enhanced in many forms. You see, the Greco-Romans considered the Paut Neteru the underworld. However; they were cannibalization, orgies, LGBT and a variety of idolatrous acts of the European form of Bosor.

Switching gears! First of all; what are the four Freedoms? They are as follows; The freedom from want, religion, fear and speech. Therefore; throughout the European Colonies (The First Amendment) was formed around 1704. Back during slavery. This is when and where criticizing the government (a slave master) was a considered a crime. Wheras; Ephesians 6:5 says "slaves obey your masters with respect, fear and sincerity of the heart as you would obey Serapis {Christ}! Serapis was created through the Greco-Romantic cult of Serapis in 3BC!

Therefore: the adjective of the word Black means a period of time characterized by tragic or disasterous events causing dispair, calamity and pessimism. Whereas; genesis 1:2 darkness was over the surface of the deep. Dark means unhappiness, tragic and calamity. As previosly mentioned in this chapter.

To whom was he speaking to and about in Luke 11:47 When he said "Woe unto you"! You build tombs for the prophets and your forefathers killed them. Ask yourselves the following; Why did your forefathers kill the prophets of old. You see, this is a continuous strategy to commit a forced form of sacratical form of genocide and total extinction of the legacy of the ancestry of the Africa heritage. This has lead to the murders of innocent individuals, blind individuals and those who are and were seeking guidance from positive role models throughout the United States of America.

These individual role models were historically renoun for their attributions and contributions towards Africa, world history and the Western Civilization. They've provided us with a legacy of the ancient African culture with their unique inventions by harmonizing societal and economical views. Views that caused anger, pain and headaches towards the European counterparts as well as the House & Field Negroe.

MENS RAE malicious aforement had and has been committed by the USA prior to and after its constitution had been reformed, reconstructed and instituted within the mainstream of modernity. This by means of all forms of slavery laws along with the current U.S Title federal criminal laws which has lead to a continuous form of ostracism and Jim Crowism.

In this; individuals have treated the lowly poorly as a result of their use of zodiac tarot and judicial astrology. This has truly been a predictable measure that lacks spiritual base. It therefore; neglects the spiritual forces that unifies all things. That is to say - the tarot practitioner in most cases has mental and spiritual infirmities that consists of the LGBT movement and are coined as frauds of political scheme. Yes, this has been a mockery of the human race at the hands of the rosecrucian cabalist. Whereas; we need a much greater form of spiritual order by all means and every sense of the word of the Metu Neter Oracle.

This world has been branded with Hades coined as a superlative form of social order. This is something to think about. They talk of a saviour. However; no one wants to die in a spiritual sense. Everyone wants the so-called necessary things stemming from their hidden agendas which are of bribery, cannibalism and barbarianisn. We as a people must recognize within our own hearts, characters, thoughts and spirits that we cannot free or save ourselves without spiritual consequence. What do you have to lose! Therefore; there's a saying "whosover shall lose his / her flesh shall be filled with the fruit of the spirit of inner-peace"!

Before Foreign Contact

European art - considered africans as savagry as they, the European organized systemic forms of cruelty as the "White Man's Degredation". This has been proclaimed as Black people have been programed to hate themselves. Whereas; Egypt knew not Pharaoh nor Israelite. This includes the Falashas - of Ethiopia as well as the Rastafarians. Therefore; before coming into contact with the explorers and invaders from the northern and westernern parts of Europe and the Asia Minor, Egypt was at peace within itself and other nations. However; through the greed of colonialism and barbarianisms the soul of Egypt had been tampered with and facimilied due to a scheme of idolatry, polythiesm and fraud!

Zechariah 11:9-10 Let those who are lefet eat one another's flesh. Then I took my staff called favor and broke it, revoking the covenant I had made with all nations. It was revoked on that day. Whereas; slavery was praised and given recognition as there is no favortism as James 2:9. Therefore; individuals tend to claim that they are highly favored by God. God is no respector of persons! In addition: Deuteronomy 28:48 Therefore; in dire, thirst and hunger, you will serve your enemies the Lord sends against you. He will put an iron yoke onyour neck until you are destroyed.

You see; the Bible was constructed by hundreds of political bigots of European monarchy. Whereas; they, the European foreknew by forseeing and developing ways of indoctrinal slavery, hypocrisy, cultural and racial barriers in their opposition towards the African rite of interrelational affairs of humanity and civilization. Therefore; one cannot have civil rights if one doesn't have human rights.

In addition; the Greco-Roman ancestry of polytheism has triggered into the mainstream of modernity. Whereas; there gods were and are sinful, murderers and are of the the LGBT movement. Their LBGT relations consisted of the following men and children. Zeus and Ganymede - a youth, Poseidon - Pelops, Sappho, Laius and Crysippus. All were lovers of idolatry and were also pedophiles. Alexander The Great was too a homosexual. Whereas; he {Alexander The Great} too had various male sexual partners. I can say the same for King David and Jonathan as well as Naomi and Ruth had a variety of lesbian encounters.

Ecclesiastes 7:26 The woman who is a trap and with a net. I find more bitter than death the woman who is a snare, whose heart is a trap and whose hands are chains. The man who pleases God will escape her; but the sinner she will snare. You see; this particular verse deals with a great deal of the philosopical and allegorical methods with regards to its biblical writings and teachings that has integrated physical and mental slavery upon the people of this modern day along with ancient Palestine, Khamit and Canaan. This also includes the fanciful story of Adam and Eve, the creation of the universe and the fall of man.

Israel, America and the entire western civilization has mocked and deludged the true rite of African marriage, family and most of: the true spirituality of spiritual love. In Europe, Israel and The United States of America - there is no spiritual union of equality in relationship and marriage. There is a dysfunctional home, nation and community within the spirit and soul of mankind. This is due to artificial and segregated forms of thinking and institutionalized education and philosophical methods of hypocrisy.

In hypocrisy, you get rhetoric which includes various movements of ungodlyness. Such as; the LGBT's, racial rioting, greed, profane lusts and pleasure-seeking politicians that promise you liberty through their wicked schemes of granduer and delusion. Truly, the woman is a snared net by western Israeli and Arabic standards. However; in African spirituality, the woman is a queen and high-priestess and an important vessal in the heart of man.

Morever; in the west, the bible, Israel and Islam they (women) are often belittled as a formed low-classed beast. The diagnosed and stereotyped African woman resides as American, Arabic and Israeli who is dependent upon the help, riches, services and welfare of the godly. This, indeed is chattel slavery at the hands of the western ways of torture. Whereas; individuals had received beatings, lynchings and victims of sodomy.

This is where the arranger has infected many with lust, greed and the lack of sharing love and understanding. People fool themselves. Therefore; in return, the Black man's heritage has been stolen after coming into contact with the conquering setien. Mark 3:27 Bind the strong man by entering his home and taking all of his rightcheous goods and wealth. They are scoffers of which has led to acts of homosexuality within the pulpits and pews of church congregations and mosques throughout the world.

You see, the bible wasn't written for the spiritual being. It was written in order to santify the ungodly. This has been successfully rendered unto many strong men by binding them into mental slavery with the woman's net (trap) / Black men have been snared in order to tranform them into becoming weak minded individuals who have been bewitched into shaming themselves. Indeed, through a web of lies. This includes the lacking esteemed motives of caretaking for themselves and love-ones as they were capable in Egypt. Whereas; western teachings by no means heal the oppressed. However; it promises wealth and prosperity for the oppressor.

Matthew 7:6 Do not give your pearls to swine. Yes, Israel and Judah are from the Canaanite culture as well as the Yemenites of the Indus Cush and The Nile Valley. You see; your spirit and soul persona are your areas of wealth. However; the Gospels and Surah are exactly what its' words are defined as. Therefore; Gossip and rhetoric are unionized and structured in order of dissuade the strong man by binding him. Tithing for what! Do not give your pearls to swine is the afore mentioned verse of Matthew 7:6. However; they live in hypocrisy of the Indo-European and many uncle-Toms and house N's. Whereas; they make every attempt to fit in within the lines of western thought and philosophy.

In addition; whenever an intelligent Black man attempt to lead a people in a positive direction. That is to say he's tormented and or murdered. You see; once again; majority of the New Testament was so-called written by Apostle Paul - Saul. Therefore; Romans 11:13 Paul mentions that he might arouse his own people as he took pride in his ministry as he spoke to the Gentiles regarding his messages pertaining to non-Jewish thought.

I've seen various flaws within Paul's messages. He too had fallen from grace, was never given grace. Saul was a murder as Paul he stole tithes, murdered and persecuted the church! Those as cunning spirits of the setien. Prior to and within Greek Old Testament times Malachi represents (messenger of Elohim) in Hebrew thought. This is to say as a reminder of ancient Israel. Whereas; they were invaders of Kemet, Palestine and Canaan.

So, my question is - / how can you give your pearls to swine as Jesus mentioned. Is this hypocrisy or what! Preachers are pimping their congregations. Those who give more receive special intercessory prayer sessions. Those who don't receive nothing but infliction, misery and sorrow. You give your more to receive your less. I disagree! Bind the strong man as written in Mark 3:27. This is through brainashing, enticement, socialism, communisn and racism.

Ancient Palestine, Khamit and Canaan were civilized civilizations of civility. They were spiritual, factual, wealthy and inhabitable places of unconditioned manifestations and devotional interrelational love. That is to say, prior to the European beligerent invaders devised schemes interfered by depopulating the African. Alex Haley's Roots was only 10% accurate in its message. We were greater than the Muslim tribes that were enslaved from West Africa who were transported to the West Indes and The United States of America.

During modern times many of our people are and have been seduced and brainwashed by the Caucasian's cleverness and schemes of producing illicit drugs and creation of unethical ways of gain. Therefore; why would you love the opressor of whom has oppressed you and your ancestors for countless generations. Zechariah 11:9 I will not be your shepard. Let the dying die and the perishing perish. Surah 17:75-77 also mentions this in similar instances! Those were the words of the Lord to Jeremiah and Zechariah 587/6 BC during and prior to the fall of Jerusalem as well as the antagonist Roman Empire.

America has copied the ways of Constantine and Ceaser by robbing African nations and African Americans. Zechariah 11:17 mentions that there were oracles used against worthless shepards for condemming Gods creation. This is contrawise to John 10:14, which was written by men of the Caucasoid race. "I Am The Good Shepard"! Therefore; this is systemic and sectional racism through syllogical and twisting forms of plagarism and chatter! Read The Metu Neter Vol I - page 359 - "How many times have you done the wrong thing while knowing what to do"?

Bind the strong man says Mark 3:27! In otherwords; they've disbarred Paut Neteru of Kemet. They've kept the Black Man and African civilization snared and entangled in slavery during their coming into contact with him. Slavery is to captivate and posess the rites of another by treachery, fraud and scheme.

You must understand that the African Civilization was and still is a wealthy and civilized civilization of interrelationalism and uniformity. However; bribery has depraved the souls of Black folk. We've created everything that exists within the histological scheme of socialism, facism and communism! They've {foreigners] twisted all positive contributions of the African ancestry. Whereas; foreign nations, European nations, Arab nations in their invasions and violations of privacy against The African people are the culprits of volunteered acts of greed and genocide.

Genocide by maiming, physical and psychological warfare have been coupled with unconstitutional affairs of spiritual and religious mockery of the ritualistic and ceremonial rites that were and are highly principaled as individuals have become one with God - their creator. This by all means has been consulted by the Rosecrucian Cabalist and masonic clergymen of fortunetelling methodologies of hypocrisy as it relates to evangelical greed and dogma.

The dogma of Christinization, Judaism and Arabization has been a creed sect amongst the underworld. The underworld includes members of the

Ku Klux Klan {KKK} -{Clergy} and the United States Government of ostracism that later created the socalled Four Freedoms throughout the era of Jim Crowism! The era of Jim Crowism has reclaimed and restored itself into the domain and mainstream of our modern ecomomy.

Africa is a wealthy civilization and holistic entity that is rich in vegetation. However; foriegn nations have brought setein possessed spirits unto its people by a constant form of controlling and hostile energies along with their beligerant arrogance, envy and hatred. This was and has been done for the economic distribution of wealth for the wealthy European and Arabizer who were and are African child molesters and child catchers. In this; they often forge death certificates from orphans and they purchase and sell children for $6,000.00 to $30,000.00. Therefore; we must first understand that possess is a state of mind and having ownership (slavery-pride-sexual exploitation -etc). It is also recognized as one who has untamed evil spirits of granduer and delusion / {psychiatrical behaviors} of negativity within one's character. Finally, it also means one being steadfast.

In addition; the African ancestry has been robbed of its possessions. Jeremiah 30:3 Write in a book the words that I have spoken to you. These days are coming; declares the Lord. When I will bring bring my people of Israel and Judah back from captivity and restore them to the land I gave their ancestors. Remember, restoration is the suffix to restore, which means to bring back to its original state or right, practice and or custom. Note; there are no chosen people. Who were the original people must be discussed.

You see; ancient Israel and Judah were of ancient Palestine, Canaan and Kemet. Neither of them incorporated or intermingled with the White Man. Therefore; whenever there's a mention of ancestry there's is also a renunciation of the practices of the nations that were within those nations. This includes the ritualistic and spiritual practices of their people. They've been considered as being of idolatry by prophets, evangelists and apostoles. Not to mention; modern clergymen and women. In this; Numbers 23:9 The Lord says, "I see a people who do not know themselves"! This too holds true. We have been blinded by pastors and co-pastors that claim to be Bishops.

Therefore; Galations 1:8-9 But even if we or an angel from heaven preach a gospel other than the gospel that we preach unto you, let them be under Gods curse. I was once under the assumption that we were redeemed from the curse of the law. Archangels are of polytheistic in nature. That is idolatry verses The Paut Neteru - which is of monotheistic with characteristics of seven personalities not gods. In addition; in that same chapter of Galatians 1 Apostole Paul mentioned that he was a specialist in Judaism. Therefore; the same is to say in Deuteronomy 17:5 as it says; take that man or woman who has done this evil deed to your city and stone them to death in front of more than one witness.

Indeed; some people are throwing you into confusion about the difference between the ritualistic spiritual practices of ancient Palestine, Canaan Kemet along with the teachings of Shechem Ur Shechem, Ra Un Nefer Amen 1 King of Kings. They would rather that you are obedient to Serapis. The god that was depicted as Greek in appearence. 322 BC. The Cult of Serapis was within Egyptologists realm of attempting to unify the Greeks and Egyptians in 3BC. This occurred in ancient Corinth. The Neolithic Corinth and the Greek god Helios was considered the sun god.

You see, polythiesm is mentioned throughout the King James Bible and Quran as sinful. However; they are followers therof; The Cult of Serapis continued throughout Sparta, Sicyon, Argos, Ermioni, Epidaurus and Laconia. The is has then become a form of Cabalistic Rosecrucian religious bigotry of which the King James Bible is written, has been written and will be preached by false prophets of this age and forevermore.

This is not sound doctrine. This is political dogma for the promotion and liberation of economic bigotry. Whereas; slavery has existed throughout the ages of universal history. Therefore; we as a people must recognize its roots and evils that has shamed the African since coming into human contact with us. The Fig Tree that was written in Hosea 9:1 and 9:10 exposes the myth of Matthew 24:32-35 where Jesus says that his words will never cease to end. In addition: Ezra 9:2 denounces the people of ancient Palestine, Canaan and Kemet. Whereas; the people of Palestine, Kemet and Canaan were considered pagans along with its neighboring nations by the Israelites who considered themselves a holy people.

Therefore; Hosea 9:1 Do not rejoice Israel; do not be jubilant like other nations; for you have been unfaithful to your God; you love wages of a prostitute at every floor. (6) Egypt will gather them (10) When I found Israel it was like finding grapes in the desert - dried up fruits of hypocrisy is exactly what they are and were. Numbers 23:9 due to their ignorance of themselves they have defiled themselves with idolatry, polytheism and darkness. They've enslaved themselves spiritually, physically and mentally through perversiveness.

Therefore; it is written; Islam, Judaism and Christianity are doomed. Whereas; their forefathers have killed the forefathers of the ancients. Luke 11:47 as they have not tombs for Jesus as well as Prophet Mohamed. There's no proof that either of the two have existed. However; there are tombs of the great people of ancient Palestine, Canaan and Kemet. There's proof. Therefore; Jesus has casted himself out! Matthew 12:26 If Satan drives out Satan he is divided against himself. You see; if there's no Satan, there's no Christianity.

Zechariah existed around 587/586 BC. as he later prophesied regarding the fall of Jerusalem to the Judeo-Greco-Romans on several instances. You see, ancient Jerusalem and Judah were once Palestine. Whereas; Palestine was Canaan. Canaan was ancient Kemet. Zechariah 11:9 Let the dying die and the perishing perish. Let those who are left eat one another's flesh. (10) Then I took my staff called favor and broke it, revoking the covenant that I had made with all nations.

In addition; the parable of the sower in Matthew 13 refers to Leviticus 26:16 where it state the following; I will bring you sudden terror, wasting diseases and fever, that will destroy your sight and sap your stregnth. You will plant seed in vain, because your enemies will eat it. I will set my face against you!

Therefore; I must say to you, what is the origin of your seed. What has triggered your negativity. What has triggered your skin color to assume that it is greater than that of the African origin. What has triggered your levels of thought. What kind of seed within you has triggered your uncontrollable temptations regarding lusts, greed, envy, hatred, deceit and racial immorality!

Well, this is a known fact that the origins of Judaism, Christianity and Islam recieved their origins from Egypt. This was then passed on by generations unto the people of Palestine, Canaan, Jerusalem and Judah. Therefore; trillions have been in servitude with regards to their lack of understanding therof. So, has your seed fallen on thorns. Have you been a hypocrate attempting to pass seeds unto the blind. Has theblind been poisoned by your false schemes of love, honesty, dedication, devotion and integrety.

Indeed, there is a substance of emasculation and effimization within this realm of religion. Religion has pondered unto the surface of destruction by all means destruction. Leviticus 26:18-19 After this; you will not listen to me. I will punish you for your sins seven times over. I will break down your stubborn pride and make the sky above you like iron and the ground below you feet like bronze. You see; this is for all modern nations as well as individuals who have failed to adhere to the ways of God. Therefore; you have fooled yourselves by bewitching others with your cleverless intellectualisms of scheme.

Jobs are what you are within every seed of Job's oppression of chapter 28. Where wisdom is found, There is a mine for silver and a place where gold is refined. (7) No birds of prey knows that hidden path. For everone is like a like a pathless bird. Therefore; slavery is within your membranes and cell walls of nuclei. Many are pathless. Many are seeking a god of lust-filled pleasure seeds. Ezekiel 3:20 Again, when a righteous person turns from their righteousness and does evil, and I put a stumbling block before them, they will die. Since you did not warn them they will die for their sin. The righteous thing that person did will not be remembered, and I will hold you accountable for their blood.

Therefore; is there really a savior. The male aspects of Seker will judge those who are dead, rebirthing and being formed! That stumbling block can be anything of your desire. However; not within the divine plan and structure of God! Not within the plan that God has for you!

Moving right along; There are wars within Kebar - Turkey - Assyria! These wars of terror have been written throughout the Holy Quran. Surah 3:151 We will cast teror of those who disbelieve, because they set up with Allah that for which He has set down no authority, and abode is the Fire. And evil is abode of the wrongdoers. As for this; there has been terrorism within the realm of Christianity, Judaism and Islam. All are negligent resulting in their stiffnecks! Jeremiah 7:25-26 from the time your ancestors entered, conquered and departed Egypt, until now, day after day, again and again. For they are a stiffed necked people who refused to listen. You people of today are a stiffed-necked people.

Therefore: Surah 3:186 You'll certainly be tried in your property {possessions} and your persons. And you'll certainly hear from those {ancestry} who has been given the book before you and from the idolaters much abuse. And if you are patient keep your duty, surely this is an affair of the great resolution. Therefore; this passage is informing the readers to stand firm in their faith for Islam as does 2 Corinthians 5:20 regarding (Christianity). It mentions the following "We are ambassadors for Christ.

You see; an ambassador is a diplomat sent by a country to represent foreign powers. Therefore; the Serapis occult has been in existence throughout the history of religion and the Rosecrucion Cabalist of the orthodoxy. This is how individuals have become canonized and indoctrinated within the so-called five fold ministry. Surah 2:30 And when the Lord said to the angels of polythiesm, I am going to place a ruler in the earth, they said: Wilt thou place in it such as make mischief in it and shed blood?

Hebrews 2:7 He was made a little lower than angels. Angels are polythiestic in nature. Yet, these religions (Christianity, Islam and Judiasm) condemn those of the ancient form. That is to say that ancient Egypt, Palestine, Canaan, jerusalem and Judah have been transformed into places of modern terror sects and locations. America too is negligent due to its poor laws on immigrations and seperate but equal laws that have been established decades prior to the end of the 20th century.

Ezekiel 3:20 I will hold you accountable for their blood! Setiens are stumbling blocks. How can you make the creator lower than angelic being if he's the creator of all things. Surah 26:29 Truly, they call the Paut Neteru {cult-gods}. However; Shechen Ur Shechem - Ra Un Nefer Amen I has ambushed the Quran, Biblical scholars and Egytologists with wisdom from God. His teachings have become a light that shines in darkness. Therefore; the Metu Neter Oracle is the Word of God.

Psalm 118:22 The stone that the builders refused shall be the chief cornerstone. Therefore; this is a reference to a king who had been disdained by neighboring slavers and bigots who had invaded his realm. In this; the Serapis Cult had received recognition for demonizing the African origin. That is how the commencing form of Judaism, Islam and Christianity rose throughout the western civilization. If history, the Quran and Holy Bible are studied with a non segregative mindset, individuals will understand where the birth of evil has its roots. For they are filled with vanities of vanity. Ecclesiastes 5:7 For a multitude of dreams and many words {there are} useless forms of hypocrisy, narcissism and conceit. You see, one cannot make himself successful through personal accomplishment and selfish achievements will not be remembered as written in Ezekiel 18:24.

Indeed, Ezekiel 21:25 it says the following; You profane and wicked prince of Israel, whose day has come, whose time of punishment has reached its climax. The dreaming and racial inequalities must cease imminently. In addition; (Hebel) {vanity} the Hebrew word means arrogance, fraud, emptiness and idolatry. This goes along to say that there are so-called scribes and political officials that claim they can make things better for the people and nations who are suffering from the lack therof; rights of humanity, social and financial equality.

Therefore; before coming into contact with foreigners Matthew 23:13 Woe to you scribes, teachers and pharisees, you hypocrates, because you devour widows houses, and for a pretense you make long prayers, therefore you'll receive greater condemnation. John 17 as Jesus prayed to be glorified is a form of hypocrisy. Therefore; read the passage for yourselves. Whereas; I previously mentiond this. For it has been written throughout the book of Ezekiel. Jesus santified himself John 17:19 Santified means {to bless thyself} make holy through {self-righteousness}. This is where individuals dream and focus on a particular diety of the TOLM yet, lack the entire understanding therof; {they lack spiritual discipline to attain spirituality} They have poor healthy conditions and untamed lusts with episodes of delusion and grandeur. Truly; these are psychological episodes of Hades and the occult of Serapis.

John 17:10 All I have is yours and all you have is mine strictly means that God is unlimited in everything and Jesus was made lower that that of angels. How then can they be one. Psalm 8:5 Whereas; if one is made lower than angels he must understand that his accomplishments are often unrecognized due to his arrogance. If an individual has a an unhealthy lifestyle, how then can he or she achieve and attain a higher form of spirituality and oneness with God and unification with all things!

Zecharia 11:9B Let those who are left, eat one anothers flesh! Whereas; in Acts 15:20 and 15:29 Apostole Paul in his debates and travels to Antioch, through Phoenecia and Samaria he encountered individuals eating meats of strangled animals that had been sacrificed and polluted unto idols. He informed the people to abstain from them. And said "you'll do well to avoin such things. You see, Paul knew better as written earlier in this chapter. Clergymen also know better. Therefore;

The Preacher Says God Is No Religion

Proverbs 17:4-7 exploits the wicked person who enjoys listening to deceitful lips. Whereas; a liar pays attention to a lying tongue. Therefore; you are only fooling yourselves. As you mock the poor and show contempt towards their Lord without having knowledge therof. This is hatred, ostracism, racism and segregation. Therefore; whoever gloats over disaster will be punished. As individuals within the church prey upon the lowly and the lower part of their being.

In this; eloquent lips are insulted to a godless fool _____ Therefore; fools fail to adhere to the wisdom of the elders. As Individuals are also intimidated by the African culture and ancestry of spirituality by all means. Truly, information does not improve one's behavior. As individuals are much worse lying lips to a ruler. Therefore; they have become followers of the rulers of darkness. They say that God is no religion. However; why then are you so-called clergymen preaching about a saviour. You see, 1 Corinthians 1:20 Where is the wise? Where is the scribe! Where is the disputer of this world. Those are sentences that one must fully recognize with regards to the nature of Christianity, western philosophy and thought. Therefore; It became pleasing to God to preach to those who believe in non-traditional forms of faith. Surah 5:18 The jews and Christians say: We're sons of Allah and His beloved ones. Therefore; the verse recognizes that the all men who follow and love God are considered to be sons of God metaphorically.

Therefore; beware of personal favortism. There is no chosen people or son! He forgives whom he pleases and chastises whom he pleases. Surah 9:30

And the Jews say that Ezra is the son of Allah: And the Christians say: the Messiah is the son of Allah. The Christian and Jewish religions were created from the pagan occult of Serapis. In addition; the jews would on no account accept Christ as saviour. Jesus Christ was never accepted by the early Jews.account.

This is a Blue-Eyed myth according to Surah 20:102 The day of the trumpet is blown, When we shall gather the guilty, Blue-Eyed, on that day! You see, these are and were the Greco-Romans. Whereas; they are a blinded people. Also, note - too - The Quran is also segregated. Truly, the Christian, Jew and Arab is radicalized in it's war against Islam along with eastern forms of spirituality by not realizing that their religion is allegorical. In this; the Christian on reads the Holy Bible for information. However; the Christian becomes holier than now and arrogant by claiming that they are highly favored. God is no respector of persons nor shows favortism. Have you not read James 2 as well as Acts 10:34. In addition; religion is being told what to do. On tthe otherhand; spirituality is the experiences of lifes endeavors

Deuteronomy 13:10 Stone them that does not believe. Yet, they preach Matthew 5:44 where it says love you enemies and pray for them who persecute you. Why then do you preach! 1 Corinthians 20-24 Where is the wise, where is the scribe, where is the disputer of this world. God has made the wisdom of the world foolish. You figure out the rest. Whereas; preaching is foolish and evil intelligence as written: verse 19 I will destroy the wisdom of the wise and bring nothing to the understanding of the prudent.

You see; clergymen have often failed to discuss ancestral rites of ancestry. They devalue ancestry of the people of color. Clergymen of color has failed its own origin. However; they discuss the geneology of Jesus. This is what has kept generations in captivity for generations. This is the sanitation of history culture and race. Therefore; if there is no Devil, there is no Christianity.

If God is no religion, what are you preaching. Why are you preaching. God is all things. However; man has used theology to save his own hind. Therefore; are you the head or the tail. The tail is the brainstem and or the buttocks. In this; there have been several forms of scheme throughout the world. In this world, John 3:16 is flawed to its root. Therefore, in Genesis Chapter 6 there were the Nephilims who were from Canaan prior to the Israeli conquest. They were called the Sons of God! They were also a massive people who were great in stature and strength. You see; gigantic is also coined as powerful and great in quality.

In addition; as written in john 3:16 God gave his only begotten son and that if all beleive they shall have have evelasing life. What happens to non-believers. The Bible was written and canonized prior to the Roman conquest of ancient Canaan and Palestine. This also includes ancient Kemet and Jerusalem / Judah. Therefore; where are the Nephilims of modernity? <<<<<<<<<<<<<<<<<<<<<<

Children Bipolar Disorder
and its Origins

Little children come unto me, and do not hinder them, say's Jesus in Matthew 19:14. To hinder means to deter and obstruct with various forms of things. Those things can be in the form of toxic chemicals, such as abusive drugs, sugars and other forms of items of enticing articles. They could also be an assortment of items that have high monetary value: such as illegal weapons -ect. Such as the following situations that occur within the Wis: Statutes:

****

948.04 Causing mental harm to a child.

948.07 Child Enticement

948.08 Soliciting a child for prostitution.

948.051 Trafficking a Child.

948..12 Possession of Child Pornography.

948.05 Sexual exploitation of a child.

948.055 Causing a child to view or listen sexual activity.

948.13 Sex Offender working with children.

984.14 Registered sex offender and photographing minors.

948.15 Other offenses against children.

a] relating to pupil discrimination.

b] relating to delivering and distributing controlled substances or controlled analogs to children.

c] relating to boxing.

d] relating to use or possession in front of children.

948.55 Leaving or storing a loaded firearm within reach or access of a child.

948.51 Hazing

Those are just a few areas that are within the Wisconsin /statutes chapter 948 regarding Crimes Against Children.

****

Moving right along. Bipolar Mood Disorder is a chronic and severe mental disability that is due to failures of the understanding of Axis 3 within DSM -V. In this, this is a result of other unresolved terminal and ancestral illnessess that individuals may have.

Such as:

1. Hepatitis

2. Cirrhosis of the Liver

3. Mitochondrial Encephalomyopathy - hypotension - central nervous system disorders -

4. Food Poisoning (eating infected foods) BSE

5. Lactic Acidosis - Aids - Cancer - Respiratory Failures -

6. intestinal Disorders - Endocrinological disturbances -&

Therefore: Bipolar's name had been so-called derived from the ancient Greek philosopher [HIPPOCRATES} Hippocrates was also known and the "father of medicine".

You see: in psychiatry DSM-V - THE SPECIFIERS FOR BIPOLAR RELATED DISRODERS MENTION;

meloncholy's features consists of the following:

1. Lack of pleasure in all or the majority of activities

2. Lack of reactivity to usual pleasurable stimuli -[its ok to be different]

3. distinct quality of depressed mood

4. excessive guilt /or inappropriate guilt / excessive arrogance and pride of not having a conscience regading others or sense of responsibilities[narcissistic disorders]

5. marked pstchomotor agitation or retardation

6. excessive weight loss / anorexia

ATYPICAL FEATURES:

1. MOOD HIGHTENS DUE TO ACTUAL OR POSITIVE EVENTS

2. EXCESSIVE WEIGHT GAIN OR INCREASED APPETITE

3. HYPERSOMNIA -

4. HYPERTENSION / RESTLESS LEG SYNDROME

5. POOR INTERPERSONAL REACTION THAT IS SIMILAR TO INDIVUALS WITH AUTISM SPECTRUM. THIS INCLUDES PEER NEGLECTFULNESS. THIS OFTEN LEADS TO SOCIAL AND OCCUPATIONAL IMPAIRMENT.

6. FEATURES OF SEASONAL AFFECTIVE DISORDERS

Therefore: [melancholy] - Melancholy has resulted in the medical diagnosing of [depression - episodes of - mania]. Melancholy also is derived within disturbances within the mitochondria. During then incubation that induces the deterioation period of the mitochondria, this welcomes the disease - encephalomyophathy.

Moving right along! Mania is related to the Greek word Menoitios, which means the following: spiritual might, might, vigorous, force and passion.

Oitios = violent, doomed and or ill-fated

Melancholy: is derived from the color within an individual's melanocytes, which means pigmentation of melanin Melanin means BLACK.

The origins of the Black ancestry is of the Egyptian, Asiatic and of African Decent. In addition: Melas was the original name of the Nile prior to the Niles inception. However: the European ancestry has little or no melanin due to their origin - being within the north of Europe. Also, true spirituality, religion, history, science and biological science reveals that individuals living nearer to the equator will always have stronger development of melanin - a darker skin color than those who are natives of the north.

Please read J.A. Rogers book titled {Nature Know No Color Line} 1980 edition. Therefore, bipolar mood disorders are secondary to encephalomyopathy, lactic acidosis and - stroke-like {episodes} [vitamin e deficiency]

Mal-an-choly is a feeling sadness with no obvious cause. This falls within the line of:

SUBSTANCE /MEDICATION-INDUCED BIPOLAR AND RELATED DISORDER DSM-V Substance / medication involved with with producing highly notable mood changes of irritablity, expansiveness, elevated or decreased appearence in mood -[mood swings] that includes features of manic or undepressed emotional state of being.

a] There's evidence from the history through physical examination and or laboratory findings that causatives have occurred.

b] There's evidence within the criterion (a) DEVOLOPED DURING OR SOON AFTER TOXINS, SUCH AS: SUBSTANCE INTOXICATION / WITHDRAWAL OR SOON AFTER EXPOSURE TO A MEDICATION.

C] BIPOLAR AND RELATED DISORDER DUE TO ANOTHER PATHOPHYSIOLOGICAL CONSEQUENCE OF ANOTHER MEDICAL CONDITION.

C1 THE DISTURBANCE ALSO CAUSES CLINICLY SIGNIFICANT DISTRESS IN THE AREAS OF THE PHYSIOLOGICAL, SOCIALOGICAL, OCCUPATIONAL, PARENTING THAT NECESSITATES HOSPITALIZATION IN ORDER OF PREVENTING HARM UPON SELF AND OR OTHERS

Symptoms of Schizophrenia
And Underlying Cause

Schizophrenia is an extremely excruciating and chronic mental deficiency. On the otherhand: many spiritualists, physicians, psychiatrists, including educators consider that individuals with this deficiency are extremely violent with various forms of aggressiveness. This incudes showing a variety of forms of abusiveness by having no understanding of themselves as well as to having the lack of regard as it relates to towards the well-being of others. This includes showing and having the extreme lack of compassion with regards to every form of God's universal plan of creation.

Truly, Schizophrenia has a variety of negative elements and disparities. Elements are divisions that are far beyond the one hundred and three elements that are witin the Periodic Table of Elements. Let's take this into serious consideration when contemplating on the sublime and subtle mechanisms that every living organism {living being} receives within his or her hemispheres that has compartments within each of the five brains.

You see, this and there are sometimes individuals who will cause harm upon others in a [clan-like fasion] by obstructing their rights of humanity as well as the right of the only True God. This is also done by the inducement of a combined usage of Chi-Electrical Manipulation. This atrocity has been geographically and geneticly triggered and are linked as disorders within the realm of phycho-pathology.

Whereas: these triggers have been inoculated for millions of years and are currently being professed through modernity while being passed unto the meager and their lower beings. Therefore: their lower beings have been affected and infected through various forms of genetic engineering through gene manipulation.

You see: the dark and deceased forces and beings rise and give birth unto the meager daily. In addition; while attempting to attain their ancestry, present and future -, they are in elemental wars of of the subliminal by opposing the positive ancestry of the living with their acts of sadism and swayisms of negatives waywardness. In addition: they temper their usage of enchantments, necromancies and cunjuration upon others. Those uses have been incorporated by and within all so-called forms of religious and spiritual practices including those that have been developed by the traditions of men. Please refer to the beginning of this topic of Schizophrenia where I am redferring to the entire second chapter of the book of Colossians.

Therefore; true intentions are often misunderstood. In many cases; there are actually true intentions of benevolence. True justice doesn't provide strategies and uses of experimental tactics in the order of producing obstructive measures as to being ujustice unto others by external and secret uses of elemental forces and powers of manipulation.

{AMP:Colossians 2:8} {Galatians 6} Therefore: see to it that no one captivate you [pseudo-intellectual babble], according to traditions and musings of mere men* The same formality has been written in Surah 16. Whereas; it says that you were made from a germ and a clot. Therefore: If you think that the idols will be involved as mediators with HIM, you are seriously mistaken, as Allah is far more intact and superior to being attached with associates.

Therefore: divisions are within each of the five brains. In addition: within each of us there is the eternal makeup along with the creation of the physiological, psychological and spiritual form of true divinity. Whereas: each individual is unique within his entire being. Therefore: with uniqueness - this also brings upon various forms of emotionional, physiological, social, psychological and spiritual challanges regarding motivational factors that includes excessive forms of stimulation with enthusiastic episodes as well as hyopotensive forms of stimuli that produces the lack of production / reproduction - thereof: You see, positive situations may consist of ritualizing and stimulating the emotional state of an individual. Therefore: this can vary within ones range of swayability, esteem, motivation and emotionality.

PSEUDAL - INTELLECTUAL BABBEL -

Pseudal is anything that is artifical and man-made. Therefore: this includes, various forms of spiritual practices. This also includes religion, liquor, uses of narcotic substances, the feeding of manufactured foods along with certain toxic vitamins and all pharmaceutical substances. These are toxic as well as psychedelic elements that produce and enhance a variety of single and combinational forms of hallucination. Hallucinations can include different stages of rage, granduer, delusion, mania, disorganized speech patterns, poor hygiene and disorganization.

In conclusion, Schizophrenia is a chronic psychiatric condition that will not only disable the disabled - it can have substantial forms of triggering mechanisms that can be extremely harmful and detrimental unto an entire population of various species, if not all. This is through genetic, spiritual, and sublimal forces. this also includes forms of psychedelic and elemental powers that all living creatures have within them internally. They are at often times victims of others usage of and practices that involve powers of manipulative genetic practices.

I TIMOTHY 5:22

DO NOT BE HASTY IN LAYING HANDS ON ANYONE

Shaken Baby Syndrome

To shake is to move or {sway} with shor or quick vibrant movements by trembling with emotion and causing the dislogment and hard fall upon an object. Whereas: a baby is a young child or animal that has not fully developed into a spiritual, physiological, mental and or physical state. You see, on the otherhand: a syndrome is a disorder, sickness, infection, disease or deficiency.

Truama becomes escalated by the above listed definitions. Head Trauma refers to abuse. Individuals with head trauma can consequently suffer from cerebral palsy and can also produce symproms of Tourette's Syndrome. Tourette's Syndrome falls within the class of Attention Deficit Hyperactivity Disorder, Obsessive Compulsive Disorder, Learning Disorders, Insomnia and TIC like movements of AUTISM SPECTRUM.

Transcient Tic Disorder is a disorder of the neurological system that can often have an affect on the autoimmune system. In this, {ENCEPHALITIS} occurs within the entire brain and circulates through the spinal column. Encephalitis incorporates with dangerous viral infections of the (STD)- (Shingel-Mump) types as well psychiatric episodes that incorporate hallucination and maniacal behavioural patterns. Also, there are uncontrollable motions and or movements of the body. This also includes -uncontrollable and untamable and abusive [outbursts]!

In addion: sudden infant death syndrome has a linkage through genetics. Therefore: the accused at often times was onece a victim of abuse in one of his / her past lives. In this, heredity, genetics / ancestry play the most important role in the lives of every living organism. Also, @ often-time, the majority of living beings and organisms haven't figured out this important truth towards their, his / her healing process.

However: if they have, the majority are conditioned within the lower spiritual and mental faculties that are within. Therefore, as a result, there are defined syndromes that have been established trough physiological, spiritual, health and mundaner laws establised to fortify and assist in the revitalizing of wholeness within all living beings as well as living organisms within themselves.

Therefore: the affects / effects of shaken baby syndrome vary with regards to severity. In this, babies often lose oxygen and its flow within the endocrine system, adreanal glands, brain and respiratory systems. Shaken Baby Syndrome is a severe form of child abuse. Child abuse is a very serious form of disregard towards humanity and the lives of the defenseless by the means of overbearingness and over-impowerment of the weak and those who are uncapable of making independent decisions and thinking for themselves.

Risk Factors

A: Lack of true culture and consistency when it comes to Environmental living standards. These standards include forms of geneticly and culturally biased based customs. Whereas: they pertain to segregated forms of thinking by its leaders and law makers. This segregated form of thinking relates to the following problems: Economics, Health Care, Welfare, Government, The Board of Education and the establishment of Religious Institutions.

B. lack of Knowledge of Self when it comes to understanding and knowing the he or she is a DIVINE BEING. In this, the aggressor will and should have the capacity of determining that his or her harmful and brutal decisions are not only harmful to self - but are harmful and or others as well. In addition, the aggressor will and should have a greater understanding that as he or she harms others - especially - the helpless child - there will be brutal consequences. This is to say, whether the consequences are enforced legally within the true spiritual community or due to karma and other forms of post traumatic stressors.

2. Lack of Self-Esteem consists of self-awareness and a humbled self-confidence as to loving, sharing, kindness and inner-peace that is liberated within all living organisms. Inner-peace that dwells from within allows an individal to make connections with his / her true towards fulfilling and mastering the {beast} negative behavioural conditions within.

Meaning, the controlling of the mammallian portion of the brain as well as the reptillian - hippocampus by connecting the dots through the entire central nervous system through a variety of forms of healing that includes [health eating habits] and holistic methods of mindfulness activities.

3. **Drugs, Alcohol and Substance Abuse** - The accused and or accuser could have been geneticly born as survivers or victims of (substance induced mood disorders). In this, AODA and other toxins have polluted humanity for millions of years. Therefore, we must cultivate the genuine form of holistic customs of truth and healing and longevity through the proper understaning proper observations of health and dietary laws. You are what you put within you!

4. **Psychiatic Disorder(s)** and the majority of one's infirmities have linkage through pathogens. These pathogens can also be induced through drug abuse and internal problems within the central nervous system as well as through the unhealthy molecular mutations of neurons, atoms and protons that are within the entire (pns) and (ans). Therefore: there can possibly an inbalance(s) within the enternal poles [Bi-Poles] of the hemispheres of the neurological system. Therefore: individuals may have a phychiatric illness due to other unknown medical conditions. This is within DMS V.

5. **Offender of Victim of Domestic Violence** can easily be swayed by another into forms of aggression due to post-partum recollections of his her negative experiences. In this, one may often place the blame upon self or upon others. Therefore, this is a transparency of individuals with anger management issues that are underlying causes of their [domestic violece issues] and current issues as they anger, arrogance aggression and high forms of stimuli that ignite derogatory and lewd forms of arousals that leads to crimes of passion, assault and murder.

6. **Genealogical history** of mistreatment of a child could also be an important factor(s) due to the individual[s} past life through pre-existence. In this, no one can exactly pin-point his / her heritage of origin. As many are indigent. Therefore, the majority of minorities are residentially housed within [the department of corrections] due to crimes against their partners, (mates) murder, and crimes against

children. This is due to the standards of the afflueza type individuals with patterns of the cognitive resonance disorder. Truly-minority populations and indigent communities are far more worse than others.

7. **Unstable family situation(s)** - Prostitution and unstable living environment often plays a major role in the compliance regards to one's accountablity with regards to applicable judicial, cultural and religious / spiritual laws that are governed by legal and religious institutions that are supposed to be governed by spiritual laws of the universe. Instability within the realms of education and employment sometimes causes individuals to stagger into perverse, lewd and vile occupations. Therefore: validity within one's spiritual awareness will have to derive from one understanding that there must be a true form of spiritual structure with training within the area of intuitiveness. This is for essentiality. therefore, while attempting towards the taming and shaping the factors of one's ;lower self, one must maintain holistic balance. Therefore; the persona must improve the self-image be self-examination through humility and being devoted to sharing and expecting nothing in return.

8. **Young and or Single Parent / Guardian** refers to immature internal anatomy as well as one's spirit and character. In this, there must be an understanding that he or she is too still a child. Therefore; the individual must be aware that the system and others will not assist you {them} if you {them} are not willing to work cohesively with others who share your passions of truth.

In addition, this is where - Immaturity plays key roles in one's every endeavor. Whether it is interpersonally, individually and or socially through true and holistic spiritual approaches. This is where western cultural affairs have harmed the meager, minorities, the weak and immature. Especially, the youth who are incapable of making their own decisions. Especially, with regards to parenting skills.

Finally, youth in western civilized nations are taught the compassion and the realization of family. They have been misdirected and guided wrongfully through television, cell phones, music and the media with patterns of demoralization by bashing members of the opposite sex and race. Therefore; there are divisive divisions that have already been established by the popular mainstream that generates racism, self-hatred, the acceptance of poverty and sexism through homonal transgressions with regards to the ill-functional health care institutions of America and the state of Wisconsin.

9. Inconsistent - Unrealistic - and Grandious Expectations of Babies through contemplation and hallucinogenic thought patterns. Mental Illness occurs sometimes through uncommon means and practices of evilness as well as toxins. Therefore: they are patterns that cause deception within one's base of reality. This leads to disappointments and failures in the long run. You see, there's no understanding with regards to the evaluation of self-standards. However, the system has various ways of establishing standards for you......

There is no regards often of one's total well-being. This means, one must become knowledgable as this pertains to his / her divinity, destiny and objectives regarding the qualities and cares and needs of the required living standards of identifying with one's true self with true cultural customs of spirituality and religion of the universal health laws the guide each of us daily.

Therefore; nothing can be unrealistic if we are aware the we too are omnipotent in our divinity. Holistic spiritual education that leads to wisdom will and should enhance an individuals healing processes and progression. Realism is knowing who you are and planning your future with a well-rounded and spiritually true {circle of friends} will enhance the progression towards to removal of regressive thought and behavioral patterns of delusion and grandiousity.

Symptoms

Poor skeletal, muscular, nervous and immune system cause the following symptoms to occur prior to and after shaken baby syndrome occurs:

COLIC - due to the digestion of dairy milk and gastroesophageal reflux disease

ANAL FISSURE DISEASE -due to anal sex (molestation)

CROHN'S DISEASE, which includes inflammatory bowel disease, bowel cancer, inflammation of the eye, anemia and tiredness.

POOR ENDOCRINOLOGICAL SYSTEM - causes difficulties to swallow and chew. Esophagitis - that induces negatives forms of situational breathing that is poor and unstable. Poor digestive tract that induces vomiting

Complications

DEVELOPMENTAL DELAYS, occur. Especially those of brittle bone disease, cerebral palsy, epilepsy and or jaundice

COGNITIVE DISORDERS AND BEHAVIORS

1. Attention Deficit Hyperactivity Disorder

2. Oppositional Defiant Disorder

3. Autism

4. Schizo-Affective Disorder

5. Schizophrenia

6. Bipolar

7. Obsessive Compulsive Disorder

8. Disruptive Disorder

9. Intrusive Disorder

10. Dissociative Disorders - with aging - Dementia, Parkinson's often and alzheimers occurs.

11. Muscular Dystrophy

12. Chronic Brain Dysfunction

All of the above listed psychiatric disordersd are located within the DSM-V from the American Psychiatric Association

---

Babies have weak trapezoid glands and muscles and can barely control their muscles. They do not have the strength due their range of growth spurts. Every child differs in his or her range and time of nurturing through the developmental stages of developnment.

In addition: if a baby is abruptly pulled by force and or sudden swaying activity, - this could lead to the following: internal bleeding - hemorrhaging within the brain and or skull simultaneously. This can also cause severe convulsive responses. Therefore: internal organs can become disjointed, have swelling, bleeding and bruising internally and externally.

Finally, please be patient with babies by not becoming easily angered due to assummed failure with regards to them not complying to you overwhelming expectations of delusion and granduer with regards to your assumptions of having failed in the attempt towards the guiding of their maturity and being properly nurtured and developed developmentally.

Do not allow negative [receptive] stimuli from others to disharmonize your progression and your dealings with children by hindering your ability of proving and showing love to others who are need of your presence.

Tejauma Na Nia Corp.

CHILD ABUSE AND NEGLECT

WIS. STATUTES

948.21

THERE'S HEALING THEREAFTER

This particular workshop defining {Child Abuse and Neglect - There is Healing thereafter - will provide a much deeper and more holistic approach towards the healing of generational and institutional behavioral modifying techniques. This workshop will also provide attendees with the availability of enhancing the physiological, spiritual and sociological beings of themselves and the children of which they are directly guiding within a child care setting.

Matthew 19:14 Jesus said the following Children Come Unto Me and Do Not hinder Them. Also, within the Holy Quran 22:5 MOHAMED spoke the words of Allah the following: "We cause What We Please To Enter The Wombs Till An Appointed Time.

Therefore: everyone must and will have clearer and holistic understandings regarding those particular passages as the two relate to the current situations of neglect, poverty, lack of love, truancy and abuse.

THEREFORE:

Definition Child: A young individual below the age of puberty or below the legal age of the majority.

Definition Abuse: To treat a person or animal violently, by the use of exploitation. Whether it be for sexual gratification or with spiritual, physical, mental and or verbally with violence. This is done in order of the abuser fulfilling his or her spiritual, sensual and or emotional pleasures of indulging in inhumane and spiritless behaviours and practices.

Definition Neglect: Failure to care for. To abandon. To disuse, deterioate and run down.

Definition: Effect. A change which is a result of an act or consequence or other cause.

The causes of Child Abuse And Neglect are due to various forms of negativity within the essential state(s) of emotionality - that lies within everyone in the world. Most importanty, an individual or individuals who have become retarded in the sense of true reality with grandeur and confusion. These realities are their lack of holistic living in nature. This also includes one or both of the following because they are known as spiritual and physiological dysfunctions in the spiritual sense. Indeed, there's a grave need of indwelling peace. In this, peace generates obedience. sharing, impariality and most importantly - LOVE and True Just.

In the physiological sense, [the list includes} there is an understanding of the entire foundation of one's own [anatomy - endocrine system - adreanal and brains resonance] self-image, character and esteem. Most importantly, one having the understanding that he or she is in non-survival mode. In knowing this, this particular being has then recognized there is no need for the use of negative forms of stimuli that triggers such vile actions and behaviour towards anyones. This includes the use of abuse of animals that includes forms of brutality and beastiality.

Therefore: this is irregardless of anyones age. In knowing this, there is no need of survival by indulging in emotional acts of abuse and neglect upon any living organism. For, survival allows individuals to act and respond upon their emotional and sensual impulses negatively unspirited. ------
This often leads to such crimes of child molestation, acts of lewdness - WI STATUTES 948.10 [exposing genitals] and forms of chronic symptoms from psychotropic medications such as: Zyprexa, Depakote, Risperdal and so on. For, they cause chemical inbalances within the dopamine inhibitors, selective serotonin reuptake inhibitors and the upper and lower hemisphers of the brain.

Indeed and truly, the following are chronic psychiatric diseases: Bipolar, Schizophrenia, Autistic Spectrum, Attention Hyperactive Disorder, Tourettes Syndrome, Post Traumatic Syndrome Disorder and Major Depressive Disorder are just a few. Whereas; they are listed in the Diagnostic Stastical Manual - DSM-V. For - they cause various forms of lewdness, yelling abruptly, grandeur, hallucinations and changes in behaviours, speech, energy, enthusiasm and mood.

This also includes perversions and profane forms of self-incriminating features of intrusiveness [Intrusive Disorder] with included forms of aggressive desires of manipulation and bullying. The child eventually becomes more traumatized and induced with {Neglect Behavior Disorder}.

Therefore, these are behaviours and defiant desires that has an oppositional effects andso-on. The desires of becoming intentional distractions through {conduct disorder - DSM} with urges of causing INTENTIONAL discomfort and displeasure unto others.

In many cases:

Adults - whether they are family members and or guardians / family friends often-times leads the child{ren} towards failing to make progression in school. Therefore; they regress. - See Wis. Stats. 948.40 and 948.45 as the 2 relate to the contribution delinquency and truancy. Therefore; these are discomforting desires of displeasure. This has gone on for millions of years throughout the world. This is beyond Zinzanthropolas of prehistoric times.

Finally, today - in modernity, I must say that this is where crimes a unto infants, toddlers, pre-schoolers and school-agers - etc has dishamonized humanity.

One must also understand that this is most oftenly an observance within indigent rural and suburban areas [by the clergy, psychiatrists and social worker

[where individuals are imprisoned, become probatinonaried and wards of the state. Indeed: there's a need for an individual and or individuals to become more holistic in nature. THIS INCLUDES EXERCISE, HEALTHY DIET, WATER AND SLEEP / REST.

Truly: they are congruent by individual(s) having one or both of the following. The first issue that becomes known is one having an unbalanced and dysfunction physiological and spiritual well-being within the understanding of self-worth and self-esteem in a holistic sense.

The second notion is that the child[ren] must be willing to learn, comprehend and cultivate his / her destablized and dysfunctional levels of the functioning of each of the brains that are within the entire brain anatomy. This happens to incorporate them into the creation of positive ANATOMICAL frequencies within his / her upper, lower, and internal organs of each of the hemispheres of the brain. This includes the eastern and western hemispheres of the brain.

Therefore; this is the reaction of dysfunctional molecular, atoms, electrons, protons, neutrons, neurons and electromagnetic life-forces of stimuli and nuclei that is either accepted or disregarded within the entire functionings levels of ones brain. ** That will be expressed and explained later**. In addition; genetic pathogens of of resonance and stimuli which has several underlying causes and effects tend to create negative forming forms of electrolytes through various sensory organs and nerves.

****

They are called some of the following;

1. Periphreal Nervous System

2. Autonomic Nervous System

3. Central Nervous System.

Let me explain this:

****

Suspected Sexual Abuse of a Child

Subsection in DCF Administrative Code 252.043 (PARENTS) see - note - section - as it relates to referral to and for special services with regards to particular need of (child-ren} - regarding special needs - and or social services activity.

Moreover: Child Care Providers, teachers and teaching assistants must be aware of applicable laws concerning and regading to children who have fallen and have been victimized through and by sexually violent and abusive persons. This is within the Wis. Stats 900 Chapter 980

The following are included within this particular are of the Statutes:

A: Definition 980.01 (1b) Act of sexual violence means - conduct that constitutes the commission of a sexually violent offense. (1d) Agency with jurisdiction means agency with the authority or duty to release or dischare the person. (4m) Serious Sex Offender, (5) Sexually motivated means that one of the purposes for is SEXUAL HUMILIATION OR DEGRADADATION OF THE VICTIM. This includes the increasing of the actor's sexual arousal or gratification or for purposes his / her id / ego to rise.

This sometimes leads to the victim generating the disorder of Gender Dysphoria. See DSM V

Moving right along ******************************

a: 980.02 - Sexually violent person petition contents - filing{s} This also includes The Entire Section of Chapter 51 Mental Health Act of The

Wisconsin Stats as it includes an evaluation (980.031) of the mental capacity of the abused child[ren] and his / her abuser. Also, in DSM-IV format of SCID-1 as relating to Axis 1

NOTE: THE ENTIRE SECTION 948 OF WIS. STATUTES [CRIMES AGAINST CHILDREN] LISTS SOME VALUABLE INFORMATION ABOUT THE IMPORTANCE AND OF UNDERSTANDING OF THE FOLLOWING: AS A RESULT OF DR. GALLO'S RESEARCH METHODS OF THE CAUSATIVES OF STD'S

1. Child Endangerment Laws

2. Child Pornography - Voyeuism - 948.055

3. Child Enticement Laws

4. Sex Offender Laws

5. Child Molestation (repeated acts of the same child) - [INCEST]

6. Rape - Molestation - that includes STD's

7. Child Prostitution - that includes STD's (teen pregnacy) THIS OFTEN LEADS TO SUBSTANCE INDUCED BEHAHIOURS IN THE OVARIES AND UTERUS. THIS ALSO LEADS TO MENTAL ILLNESSES THAT ARE DUE TO OTHER GENERAL MEDICAL CONDITIONS [DSM -IV PAGE 165.

8. Sex Trafficking - that includes the formulation of STD's

9. Physical Abuse of a Child - By promoting arious acts of bullying

10. Having sex with children and the furnishing of alcohol to a child - and promoting (chrystal-meth) and other forms of drug paraphenalia in the presence of a single child of child[ren] through sex-trafficking in the following world-wide locations

1. India

2. South Asia -

3. South America

4. The UK

5. The eastern and western portions of the USA

6. West Africa, Senegal, Nigeria, Niger and South Africa

7. The East Indes

11. Promoting acts of Bullying

_____

_____

_____

DSM There Is Help

With and true and holistic cultured cultivated forms of living standards along with proper guidance that includes a calm, peaceful and loving home-living atmosphere, the child[ren] will begin the atoning their path of rejuvenizing and revitalizing the purpose that The True God has provided.

In this, the learning environment has to be induced with proper and true holistic measure with forms of structured behavioral modifying methods. This includes true forms of [MINDFULNESS -ACTIVITIES] - Also, with proper forms of evaluational techniques of Holistic Mainstreaming Procedures that incorporates all cultures, - not just a few.

CHILDREN, AS WELL, IN SOME CASES, IT MAY BE THE THE PARENT(S) WHO HAS UNKNOWINGLY AFFECTED THE CHILD / CHILDREN THROUGH HIS / HER DNA - RNA STRANDS.

MAINSTREAMING

and well as a close and safe family net along with support from Guardians, Child Care Providers, Teachers, Teaching Assistants, Social Services, Community Organizers, Local Government Agencies and Clergy should provide individuals with a safe haven of love. They should also play key roles in assisting them in enhancing their strong sense of encouragement, union and social harmonious forms of peace. Inner peace that includes the knowledge of loving ones self, having the love for others and internal shelter within their own spirit-beings. This is the sense and urge of inner peace which is the true meaning of peace that nothing in the world can violate.

Finally,

We truly are divine beings. Therefore; with just and true love, we must be examples of excellence unto every living being of which we have interactions - especially children. We must also learn and accept that we too as teachers and leaders must be willing to be humbled learners of holistic truths by incorporating them within the totality of our beings.

****
****

As mentioned in the opening: matthew 19:14 Let the little children come unto me - and do not hinder them. This includes Surah 22:5 We cause what we please to enter the wombs till an appointed time.

Lets remove the shackels of darkness and see through the light of unconditionalism and love. Know your divinity.

Thank you all and God Bless.

Fetal Alcohol Syndrome

Fetal Alcohol Syndrome relates to the so-called human embryo of an unborn that is within a rudimentary stage with the potentiality of the enhancement of stages of growth and development. This can also mean the following: immature, underdeveloped and incomplete or premature. This occurs as a result of pregnant mothers having excessive usage of alcoholic substances as well as other drugs that are harmful to the unborn fetus. This disorder also has a genetic linkage. Therefore: as a result of {Fetal Alcohol Syndrome} The following disorders occur:

a} Physiological - Neurological - ENDOCRINOLOGICAL

* CNS

* PNS

* ANS

* SNS

1. Sensory Development Dysfunctions

2. Poor motor development * Sugar Diabetes - Cirrhosis - COPD

3. INTERNAL ORGAN DISORDERS - {WILL BE EXPLAINED}

b] Psychiatrical -

learning and cognitive disorders that includes the following anxiety and behavioral disorders

1. ADHD

2. Schizophrenia - or Schizo Affectiveness

3. Bipolar I or II

4. Dissociative Disorder

5. Oppositional Defiant Disorder

6. Intrusive Disorder

7. Autism

c] Physical Disturbances occur;

1. Anorexia

2. Bulimia

3. Chronic Brain Dysfunction (cerebral palsy)

4. Skull fractures

5. Malformations within the facial features

6. Pre-natal / Post natal deficiencies

7. Genital Anamalies

8. Joint abnormalities {RLS}

9. Dwarfism - CNS - MICROCEPHALY

d] Endocrinological Disturbances

1. Sugar diabetes

2. Cirrhosis of the liver,

3. COPD

4. Heart Murmors

5. Anemia

6. Vitamin Deficiencies - WILL BE EXPLAINED

CORPUS CALLOSUM DISORDER SYMPTOMS INCLUDES:

Dysfunctions within the cerebral hemispheres of the brain leading to some of the following:

1. Gender Dysporia:

2. Transvestic Disorder

3. Leads to {Escoriation Disorder} with suicidal tendencies

4. Epileptic Seizures

Fetal Alcohol Syndrome relates to the embryo of an unborn having various forms of deformalities due to pregnant mothers having excess and excessively using toxins. Such as: cigarettes, caffeine, marijuana, opium, crack co-caine, herion, alcoholic substances while they are pregnant. This also includes the males history of substance usage as this relates to {TRANSGENIC ORGANISMS} Whereas: transgenic modification is accomplished inserting any form of DNA into an embryo. Therefore:

male sperm, as it enters the uterus and ovarian section after entering the vagina this can also lead to the transferring of unclean cells containing {organisms} that consists of deadly infections and STD's.

This then causes various forms of cancers and std's. However; I will only mention a few. The list includes the following: The (EHV) Equine Herpesvirus Myeloecephalopathy - [spinal- brain blood disorders} as well The Human Papillomavirus, Aids, HIV, Colorectal Cancer, Pancreatitis - Cancer, Lung Cancer, Anal Cancer, Gall Bladder and Cirrhosis of the Liver.

Finally, in conclusion: I ask that everyone understand the various dangers and hazards as they relate to Fetal Alcohol Syndrome. Fetal Alcohol Syndrome is a syndrome of pathogenesis within the cause of humanity and all species. Therefore, please be mindful that the linkage of genes can be passed on as psycho-magnetic energies of uncleanliness that leads to human disparity and depopulation of all of the true and remaining healing mechanisms towards everyone's post-developmental stages of spiritual, emotional and physiological divinity.

Where there is pain and suffering that includes depression and anxieties that causes {FAS} - There is also healing and knowledge. The knowledge base of cultivation within one's eternal soul is providing a strong safety-net to anyone. For, this is the most beautiful and nurturing thing there is to be accomplished and fulfilled within the universe. Just be true to yourself by finding your divinity and that one that's within your undeveloped fetus.

Autism Spectrum

MODERN RESEARCH AND SO-CALLED SYMPTOMS AND CAUSES OF AUTISM SPECTRUM:

SYMPTOMS: In psychiatry, the spectrum of autism and its symptoms include a variety of deficiencies that includes the following.

1. Speech and language barriers - such as slurred speech and infirmities within portions of the cerebral cortex brain. Through neurobiology and by having knowledge that is based on the (sns) sensory nervous system regarding stimuli that the cerebrum receives in order of the enhancing the proper maintenance of intrapersonal relationships in all living beings and organisms. By mastering the understanding, this will then allow individuals with AUTISM - SPECTRUM DISORDER to remove idlesness from within their physiological persona and spiritual anatomy and become independent / interdependent individual by being more holistic in nature.

2. Repetition Compulsive Behavior(s) - the recurrment of an activity or an event. This leads to Post Traumatic Syndrome Disorder {seeking revenge}

a. Peer Neglect

b. Social Anxietiy

3. Behavior Reinactment Disorders.

4. Developmental Disorder {Gross Motor Disorder}

Is caused by disorders within both the MOTOR CORTEX & the PRE-CENTRAL GYRUS which are regions within the cerebral cortex. This causes disoriented skills in the areas of movement [inappropriate verbal and bodily gestures] with poor coordination within one's arms, legs and other large parts of the body.

A. Cerebral Palsy Occurs unless there is an intensed for of physical and or aquatic therapy

5. Developmental Disorder {Fine Motor Disorder}

A. Stages of Development are unbalanced that includes malformations within the muscles of (hands-feet). This also includes the [cns} central nervous system. This can also cause one or each of the following deformalities to occur: MS, Spinal Bifida and Down Syndrome.

ALSO,

5. Gastrointestinal Systems [various]

6. Sensitivities to loud sounds and noises

7. Gender Dysporia - Gender Identity (DSM -V) will be explained through the following examples;

Conjugation Chromosome - DNA that can exist as a plasmid or become integrated into a chromosome. This delivers chromosomal genes unto another species with pure accuracy. This is the (HRF-Cell) -homogolus recombination cell - produces gender transforming genes unto individuals. This then affects ones entire physiological state of being by tranforming them into individuals with a variety of identity and personality disorders that are described in all volumes of the DSM.

Transgenic organism - is an organism at is and has been modified with genetic material from another material from another species. The genetic modification is acomplished by inserting DNA into an embryo with the assistance of a **{VIRUS}**, a plasma or a gene gun! The embryo is then allowed to develop. Then mature organisms will express the DNA which has been inserted into its genome. Transgenic organism can also pass the modification on to [FUTURE GENERATIONS] of CHILDREN. WHEREAS: GENES ARE ALWAYS TRACED TOWARDS ONES ANCESTRY OR ANCESTRY OF AN ILLNESS / ILLNESSES - by breeding with other members of the same or different species.

HISTORY, ORIGIN AND TRUE UNDERLYING CAUSE:

a. Drug Abuse during pregnancy by one or both of the parents during each tri-master

b. Receptivity to Toxins and chemicals. This also includes, tobacco usage, herion usage, crack - cocaine usage - opium usage and Alcoholism during pregnancy.

c. Malnutrition. This can also be the result of a genetic pathogen that is linked the ancestry.

d. Immunizations and Infections such - as veneral diseases [STD's] during pregnancy

---

3. Folate Deficiency - Folate is a B9 vitamin that often includes the need of B-12 -This helps to maintain a balanced heart rate, proper blood circulation and induces assistance for the enhancement of both - the motor and sensory nerves. Finally, B-12 and Folate B-9 if used congruently will treat anemia [cns / respiratory woes] properly that is caused by both - B-12 and folate acid deficiency. The two will is also used ro prevent neural tube disorder.

Who has bewitched this generation and past generation - along with future generations through the recreation of transgenic organisms. A transgenic organism is an organism that has been modified with genetic materal from another species. The genetic modification is accomplished by inserting DNA into an embryo with the assistance of a virs, a plasma or a gene gun. The embryo is allowed to develop and the nature organism will express the DNA which has been injected into its GENOME.

Transgenic organisms can also pass the MODIFICATION on to the future generations by breeding with others of the same species. This also includes chemical toxins, bee stings, snake venoms, dog bites and feces from other living organisms.

Therefore: The heritability of autism deals with conjugation chromosome through the complexed scientfic methods of TRANSFORMATION GENDER. In this, methods {DNA} from one species can have full expression within another. Therefore, Many Organisms are genetically modified. Many animals, which too are organisms have too been geneticly modified as their DNA has been induced into humanity - through usage of [gene guns].

In this, {TRANSGENIC MONKEYS were introduced to the world thousands of years ago. Whereas: this is factual and generational. As [SIMIAN IMMUNODEFICIENCY VIRUS] existed in hundreds of species in African non-human primates. This also includes monkeys from [bioko island] nearly 12,000 years ago. Whereas: (SIV) has been present in monkeys and apes for more than 32,000. American Biomedical Researcher, Dr. Robert Charles Gallo claims to have mentions dicovered the aids virus in humans in 1984.

In addition, and finally, in an article written on 1-25-2016 written be Antonio Regalado, it mentions that scientists in China say they used genetic engineering to create monkey with a version of autism. The research was done by neuroscientist Zilong Qi of the Shanghai Institutes of Biological Sciences. Qi say "{The monkeys show very similar behaviours (human autism patients). Whereas: it damaging effect to the MECP2 GENE CAUSES Rett syndrome in girls.

Finally, e Holy Quran on Embryonic Development mentions the following in Al-Mu-minUm: The Believers - Surah 23:12-14

and certainly We created man from an extract of clay. Then We made him like a small germ in a firm resting-place. The We make the life-germ a clot, then We make the clot a lump of flesh, then We (in) the lump of flesh bones, then We cloth the bones with flesh. then We cause it to grow into another creation.

Therefore: Autism has to be observed more patiently. Whereas; it has many affects upon the shape of the lives of an entire population of humanity. True individuals that love children will be successful with patience and enduring love and modest understanding of the lives of others in their dealings with individuals with all forms disabilities will be impressively blessed.

SIDS Sudden Infant Death Syndrome

Definitions: of sudden, infant and death!

SYNDROME(S) - ARE GENERATIONALLY INHERITED FROM STRANDS OF DNA AND RNA ALONG WITH RACIAL AND CULTURAL LINES THAT INCLUDES [HEALTH]BARRIERS] THROUGH [BLOOD-LINE] - [HUMAN CONTACT] AS WELL AS THROUGH PATHOGENS THAT INCLUDES A VARIETY OF TRIGGERING FORMS THAT IGNITES THE {TOXIC SHOCK SYNDROME} THROUGH ELECTROMAGNETIC FACTORS OF STIMULI.

SUDDEN - something clearly that is recognized as being out of the blue, unanticipated and unforeseen. Those situations are usually seen as situations that can have defects, affects and effects on an individuals total holistic health and well being.

DEATH - They say that this is the end of life of an organism.

INFANT - is a young child, infant or baby

LYSTERIA MONOCYTOGENES:

Lysteria Monocytogenes was so-called first discovered in Nova Scotia, France in 1924 by E.G.D. Murry based on sudden deaths in rabbits prior to Harvey Prile changing its name to Lysteria in 1940. causes 2,500 illnesses and 500 deaths per year based on CDC. There have been reports 1/3 of deaths involve pregnant women that had miscarriages within their fetuses. This disease is caused by the feeding and earting of cold cuts. Neonatal Infections often occur as well due to the child contracting and bearing virusus such as: HIV, HEPATITIS B and MALARIA

Also, beta-casomorphin-7 is a peptide that is produced in baby formula that has been linked to sudden infant death syndrome. An enzyme named dipeptidyl peptidase-IV or DPPIV -modified as 7causes Sleep Apnea and eventually and suddenly attacks one's {an infants} brainstem. This causes {Sudden Death Syndrome}

However: everything along with every living organism has to die and become something else or something better than it was previoulsy. This is considered reincarnation and resurrection by western philosophy and religious thought.

However: this is considered creation, death, regeneration and rebirth by standards of many modern religions as well as many ancient eastern cultures and civilizations.

Therefore: toxins harm and disharmonized the (cns) central nervous system. Fetal Alcohol Spectrum is a disorder that occurs within the mother during the periods of pregnancy and lactation that is the result one of the parents having an addiction to alcohol.

A toxin is an antigenic poison or venon of plant or animal origin, especially one that is produced or derived from microorganisms when present at low concentrated levels within the body.

An antigenic is a toxin or foreign substance which induces immune response with the body, especially the production of antibodies. Whereas; venoms are substances that are produced by dangerous creatures such as, snakes, serpents, scorpions and bees that is most often injected into prey.

A prey is something that is hunted, haunted in order of being harmed by torture or suddenly murdered. Therefore, microorganisms are germs, ailments, infirmities, bacteriums, illnesses, infections, diseases, viruses, conditions and disorders.

In most cases; they are caused by toxins. In all cases; the following toxins cause forms of sudden death slowly within the womb during the early stages of prenatal development:

1. Tobacco Withdrawal, which is commonly known as Tobacco Use Disorder. Smokink increases perinatal problems, such as low birth rate and miscarriages within the areas of comorbities of DSM V. Tobacco use also induces psychiatric disorders such as major depressive disorder, bipolar and anxiety.

Alcohol use also deteriorates the nicotine inhibitors within the brain and slowing destroys the oxygen levels withion the kidneys and lungs. It also deduces the Nicotintic Acetylcholine Receptors in humans. In humans, at the neuromuscular junction for muscle and nerve muscle communication.

If communication levels deteriorate within the cerebellum, the receptors become il-functionable by causing musculoskeltal problems and disharmonizing forms of proper muscle contraction within the immune system.

The immune system, autoimmune system consists of the colon, prostrate, pancreas, liver, anus, rectum - {BLADDER} - gall bladder. If the use of venomous toxins which includes the eating of processed foods are warranted the following diseases and ailments can and will eventually occur and have lethal effects on the unborn throughout perinatal stages:

A: CIRRHOSIS

B: DIABETES

C: ENURISIS - LOSE BOWEL -

BLADDER INFECTION, DUE TO UTI = URINARY TRACT INFECTION WHICH EVENTUALLY BECOMES COLON AND OR PROSTRATE CANCER

D: ENCOPRESIS -LOOSE BOWEL AND OR CONSTIPATION

E: IBD

F: HIV

G: AIDS

H: and s-on.

In the Holy Quran's Chapter as it relates to portions of The Pilgrimage and portions of Surah 22:5 - it mentions the following:

we created you from dust, then from a small-like germ, then from make clear unto you: And we cause what we will to enter and remain the wombs until an appointed time.

We bring forth as babies, then that you may attain your maturity. AND OF YOU, HE IS CAUSED TO DIE!

Similar instances occurred are within The Holy Bible and Torah as it relates to King Herod in {Syria} wanting to kill Jesus in Matthew Chapters 1 and 2.

Also, note within the Book of Exodus 11:5 (every first born boy in Egypt shall Die within every house-hold) orders were given by the so-called phaorah in Egypt unto the trading and slaving Northern European Jews and Native Egyptians.

Moving right along. The cerebellum, which controls muscle movement and coordination. In this, cerebellar degeneration occurs when the cerebellum begins to slowly deteriorate and die which causes lithium and Vitamin D deficiencies. Lithium is used in patients with psychiatric disorders that coinside with manic episodes of delusion that eventually leads to [DISSOCIATIVE DISORDERS] see: DSM V.

Now to make it clear, the Nicotinic Acetylcholine Receptor is also diverse and destroyed through the following:

1. Peripheral Nervous System

This particular are consists of the Ganglia and spinal cord. This also consists of the Autonomic Nervous System and the Somatic Nervous System.

The AUTONOMIC NERVOUS SYSTEM consists of the following: the heart, digestive system and arousal state in living organisms. While the SOMATIC NERVOUS SYSTEM consists of SENSORY NERVES AND MODES OF REFLEXION.

2. SYMPATHATIC NERVOUS SYSTEM

The Sympathatic Nervous System consists of rate of blood pressure within the Central Nervous System and the gastrointestinal tract - which includes the {immune system} of the enteric nervous system of the muskuloskelen system.

3. PARASYMPATHETIC NERVOUS SYSTEM

Parasympathetic Nervous System consists of nerves within the ears, partitoid {salivary glands} from the intake of {food starches}. The PNS also includes regions of ovaries, uterus, uterea, pelvic region and the cervix as it relates to movements within the cervical spondylitite muscles within the spine of the neck region of the TRAPAZOID - TRAPIZIUS.

You see, In insects, the cholinergic system is limited unto the Central Nervous System. Therefore, the cholinergic system as it relates to various sodiums that are within animal tissues. That substance contains N, N, N - which is known as trimethylethanalammoniumcation. N, N, N affects the neurotransmitters and the central nervous systems congruently by either receiving too little or more than the actual need of {LECITHINl} and {INOSITOL}

LECITHIN - is derived from egg yolks, cooking of of petroleum and polyurathane that is a form of ammonia and paint enhancing acrylic resins.

INOSITOL - is commonly used in patients with depression, schizophrenia, panic disorder, diabetes, anxiety, obsessive-compulsive disorder, polysistic ovary syndrome and or diabetis during pregnancy.

You see, the central nervous system and the neurotransmitters work cohesively within the neurotransmissions within the brain to resolve holistic issues within in individuals physiological being in order of producing results of healing wholesomely and holisticly:

*** NOTE THE EXAMPLES BELOW ****

Neuroadrenergic Pathways and Origins for example are:

THE PRODUCTION OF ENCEPHALITIS DUE TO THE FOLLOWING:

0. Viral Infections

1. Inflammation of the brain

2. HIV - AIDS

3. Autoimmune Deficiencies

A. Amygdala / hippocampus / reptillian

B. Brain stem and spinal cord - Oblongata

{RESPIRATORY SYSTEM}

C. Cerebellum

D. Cerebral cortex

E. Thalamus - Hypothalmus

F. Tectum

G. Ventral Tegmental Area

THE REGULATION OF COGNITIVE PROCESSES AND BEHAVIORS

A: Anxiety

B: Arousal

C: Negative Emotion Memory

D: Rewards within a reward system

E: Cognitive Control and Working Memory

F: Negative - Receptive - Stimuli

You see, toxins surround us daily. Whereas: we are constantly being pulloted with toxins daily. The children are facing health challanges prior to them entering wombs and ovaries. {Deutoronomy 28:61}

Toxins for procedures in [pregnancy and lactation] medications has led to millions of deformalities, defects and forms of abortions and sudden deaths in infants.

PARABAN - is used the form of a fertility drug for women. Therefore; here is an example. Whereas: it is an endocrine disrupter and has been associated with:

- Attention Deficit Disorder

- Learning Disabilities

- Cognitive Disorders

- Brain Development Problems

- Deformation of the Body -Limbs

- Breast Cancer, Thyroid Cancer, obesity,

and Diabetes

- Female Reproduction System by-

Masculizing Females

- Male Reproduction

Feminizing Males

****

TOXINS IN CANNED FOODS

Bisphenol is a form of polycarbonic plastic is found in the majority of canned foods

Metabolic Disease of Thyroid Cancer

Hormone Diseases

Neurological Diseases - including manic episodes, depression, anxiety and hyper-activity within the central nervous system.

Asthma

Luekemia

Breast Cancer(s)

Gender Identity Disorder - that involves the development of poor and inconsistent estrogen levels

Baby Formulas Promote Lysteria Causing Sids Sudden Infant Death Syndrome

DEFINE:

SUDDEN -

INFANT -

DEATH -

www.ingramcontent.com/pod-product-compliance
Lightning Source LLC
Chambersburg PA
CBHW050414290526
45786CB00003B/1263